Fodor's InFocus

CAYMAN
ISLANDS

Welcome to the Cayman Islands

This British Overseas Territory is almost as well known for its banks as for its breathtaking beaches and vibrant coral reefs. But excellent hotels, a broad array of vacation condo and villa rentals, and fabulous restaurants keep visitors coming back. This book was produced in the middle of the COVID-19 pandemic. As you plan your upcoming travels to the Cayman Islands, please confirm that places are still open and let us know when we need to make updates by writing to us at this address: editors@fodors.com.

TOP REASONS TO GO

★ **Diving:** Underwater visibility is among the best in the Caribbean, and nearby reefs are healthy.

★ **Safety and Comfort:** With no panhandlers, little crime, and top-notch accommodations, it's an easy place to vacation.

★ **Dining Scene:** The cosmopolitan population extends to the varied dining scene, from Italian to Indian.

★ **Fabulous Snorkeling:** A snorkeling trip to Stingray City is an experience you'll always remember.

★ **Beaches:** Grand Cayman's Seven Mile Beach is one of the Caribbean's best sandy beaches.

Contents

MAPS

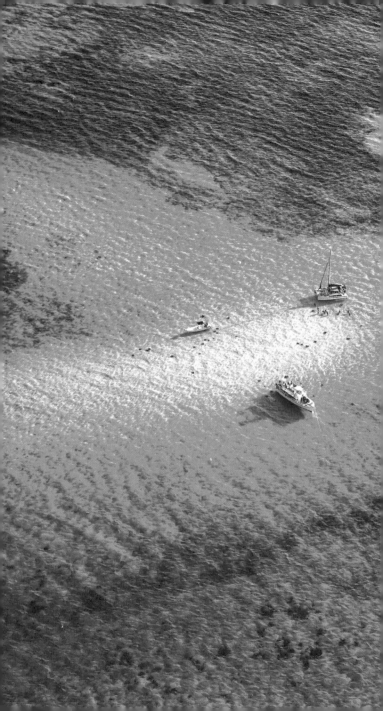

Chapter 1

EXPERIENCE THE CAYMAN ISLANDS

18 ULTIMATE EXPERIENCES

The Cayman Islands offer terrific experiences that should be on every traveler's list. Here are Fodor's top picks for a memorable trip.

1 Seven Mile Beach

Those who love long, broad, uninterrupted sweeps of champagne-hue sand will be thrilled with Grand Cayman's longest beach. *(Ch. 4)*

2 Bird-Watching on the Sister Islands

Bird-watching on the Sister Islands Booby Pond on Little Cayman and the Brac's Parrot Reserve are just two of the gorgeous areas set aside for communing with nature. *(Ch. 7, 8)*

3 Buying Crafts on Cayman Brac

Some of the best local craftspeople, including Annalee Ebanks (thatch-weaving) and Tenson Scott (Caymanite carving), are found on the Brac. *(Ch. 7)*

4 Shopping in George Town

In addition to dynamite duty-free shopping, the handsome waterfront capital hosts the historic Cayman Islands National Museum. *(Ch. 3)*

5 Cayman Crystal Caves

Cayman Crystal Caves are spectacular, surrounded by a lush tropical forest in Grand Cayman's Old Man Bay. Formed over millions of years, they are still continuing to evolve. *(Ch. 6)*

6 Dine at Blue by Eric Ripert

The wine-pairing menu at Le Bernardin, chef Eric Ripert's only Caribbean restaurant, is the kind of epicurean experience that comes along once in a blue moon. *(Ch. 5)*

7 Happy Hour in George Town

Such popular waterfront spots as Rackam's and The Wharf serve creative cocktails and reel in the revelers for sunset tarpon feeding. *(Ch. 3)*

8 Queen Elizabeth II Botanic Gardens

Critically endangered blue iguanas have found a home at this park, where you learn about their life cycles, then stroll the peaceful, gorgeously laid-out gardens. *(Ch. 6)*

9 Diving the Kittiwake Wreck

One of the best-known wreck dives in the Caribbean is just off the Seven Mile Beach shoreline; only 60 feet down, it teems with vibrant marine life. *(Ch. 4)*

10 Listening to Barefoot Man

Head to the Wyndham Reef Resort in East End to hear the blond Calypsonian, Barefoot Man (née George Nowak), a beloved island icon. *(Ch. 6)*

11 Taste the Local Food

Sample mouth- and eye-watering jerk chicken from a roadside stall or George Town shack. A few local chefs even serve meals in their homes. *(Ch. 3)*

12 Owen Island

Easily accessible by kayak from Little Cayman's "mainland," Owen Island appeals to snorkelers and romantics, who have their choice of captivating coves. *(Ch. 8)*

13 Bloody Bay Wall

One of the top dive sites in the world plunges from 18 feet to more than a mile into the Cayman Trench; the visibility is remarkable. *(Ch. 8)*

14 Cayman Batabano

The biggest Carnival celebration in Cayman has been rocking George Town during the first week of May since 1983. *(Ch. 2, 3)*

15 The Perfect Spa Day

Pamper yourself at one of the swanky resort spas on Seven Mile Beach. The Ritz-Carlton offers quiet zones and elaborate treatments to melt your worries. *(Ch. 4)*

16 Grand Cayman's Bioluminiscent Bay

The bio bay in Cayman Kai is one of a few in the world. Witness the water glow bright blue in the dark as tiny organisms wriggle and shimmer radiance. *(Ch. 6)*

17 Horseback Riding on the Beach

Ride a gentle, well-trained horse along Cayman's most pristine remote beaches and nature trails. Choose from morning, afternoon, sunset, or moonlight horseback rides. *(Ch. 3, 5)*

18 Stingray City

You can interact with gracefully balletic, silken stingrays, so "tame" you can feed them as they beg for handouts on this shallow sandbar in the North Sound. *(Ch. 6)*

WHAT'S WHERE

1 George Town. The country's mesmerizing and rich capital is steeped in history and awash with pastel-color buildings offering duty-free shopping, charming coffee shops, waterfront dining, and historic sights.

2 Seven Mile Beach. Sandwiched between dazzling cyan waters and dense green foliage, Seven Mile Beach is lined with swanky resorts and great restaurants, all offering front-row seats to the famed sunsets.

3 West Bay. With crystalline waters and beaches that quite literally sparkle, the district is packed with popular attractions, delightful Cayman cottages, and white-sand beaches.

4 North Side and East End. Cayman Kai and Rum Point in the eastern districts offer a gateway to hidden crystal coves peppered with starfish, deliciously warm waters, the majestic Crystal caves, and the must-see bioluminescent bay. Farther out, the East End is where locals live.

5 Cayman Brac. This slow-living escape is a mecca for divers and nature lovers floating 90 miles (143 km) northeast of Grand Cayman.

6 Little Cayman. Beat the crowds by visiting the most under-the-radar of the three islands, famous for its idyllic tranquillity and vibrant reefs.

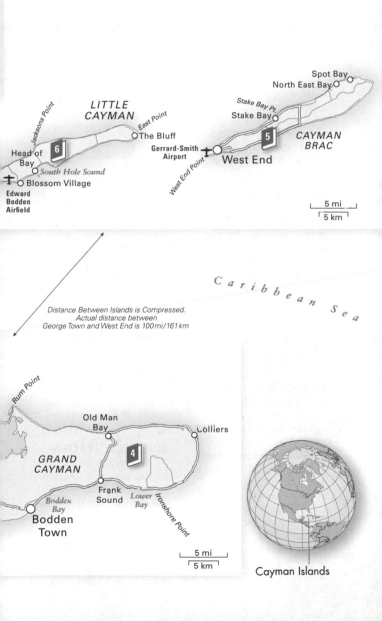

Spot Bay

North East Bay

Stake Bay Pt.

Stake Bay

CAYMAN BRAC

5

Jacksons Point

LITTLE CAYMAN

East Point

The Bluff

Gerrard-Smith Airport

West End

West End Point

Head of Bay

South Hole Sound

Blossom Village

Edward Bodden Airfield

5 mi
5 km

C a r i b b e a n S e a

*Distance Between Islands is Compressed.
Actual distance between
George Town and West End is 100 mi/161 km*

Rum Point

Old Man Bay

Colliers

GRAND CAYMAN

4

Frank Sound

Lower Bay

Ironshore Point

Bodden Bay

Bodden Town

5 mi
5 km

Cayman Islands

Welcome to the Cayman Islands

Glistening seascapes frame a spectrum of glorious white beaches in the Cayman Islands. Luxurious resorts line the sparkling coast, bleached by endless sunshine and happy-go-lucky locals, although COVID-19 saw the island shut its borders to visitors for much of 2020, the country's unique charm hasn't faded in the slightest.

Professionals and digital nomads can embrace a remote lifestyle and immerse themselves fully in the beauty and culture of the Cayman Islands. The Global Citizen Concierge Program allows for approved digital nomads to live and work remotely on a beautiful island paradise for up to two years in this carefree corner of the Caribbean. Once it's safe to welcome sun-seeking travelers to its shores once more, it will.

THE BEACH IS JUST THE BEGINNING

An island getaway to Grand Cayman will surprise you with a captivating fusion of old and new. There's an ease of living here brought on by the infectious, relaxed attitude that wafts through the sea air. The tranquil lapping of the sea against the shore and a "Caymankind" ethos, which isn't merely uttered, but lived. If lazing and soaking up the sun isn't for you, you're in luck, here the beach is just the beginning.

The capital George Town, with its colorful boats docked at the picture perfect harbor, offers an eclectic blend of cultures, duty-free shops, and attractions, while to the west and east you'll find secluded bays, charming characters, and fishermen floating happily in the cool waters. Hike through exotic brush, wade through magical, glowing waters, or ride on horseback on a secluded bay—whatever you decide to do, Grand Cayman is packed with as much or as little action as you desire.

Much of the capital has been pedestrianized so you can meander through the streets, and with development more rampant than ever, new hotels with a focus on wellness, including the Kimpton Seafire and Palm Heights, and soon-to-be-built Hilton and Hyatt bring more amenities than ever before.

MULTICULTURALISM

Spend a day in the buzzing capital, and you'll see workers from every corner of the globe darting back and forth from offices and coffee shops. The Cayman Islands has fast become a mecca for expats, with 135 different nationalities replacing metro stations and skyscrapers with soothing seascapes and lofty palm trees. The combination of social events, oceanfront serenity, and a luxurious life-style is part of Grand Cayman's heart and soul. Now more than ever, the island caters to a diverse range of interests and tastes, with new restaurants, bars, and shops popping up monthly. Job opportunities exist for young professionals wanting to develop their trade and nurture their careers while experiencing a quality of living you'd be hard-pressed to find anywhere else on the planet.

POLITICS

Caymanians love to talk about politics, and in any election year the focus will be on health care, economic development, and education, particularly after months of lockdowns during COVID-19. The current party in power, the PPM have seen 59-year-old Alden McLaugh-lin lead them through the pandemic while serving his fifth term in the Legislative Assembly.

WHAT CAYMANIANS ARE TALKING ABOUT

It's not always sunny in paradise, and Caymanians love nothing more than to chat about the weather. The Cayman Islands do enjoy a very warm, tropical climate year-round, with temperatures reaching up to 91°F in the summer months, but hurricane season runs from June through November, and each year several topical depressions and even hurricanes pass over or close to the islands. The National Weather Service gives plenty of warning if a storm is on its way, and local stores and news outlets do a good job of making sure you know how to stock up for the season in preparation for the worst.

More recently, the conversations have drifted toward the controversial topic of tourism recovery and the continued growth and development of the islands. If Cayman's popula-tion resumes its pre-COVID growth rate, the island will be home to 100,000 people by 2031. An analysis of population trends by civil servant Dr. Philip Pedley, published in 2007, examined past trends and future possibilities. As Pedley wrote, "How will the popula-tion of Cayman change in the next 20 years? The question has important implications for every area of government policy and public life—from the number of schools needed to demands on the healthcare system to environmental, social, and infrastructure pres-sures to the size of the George Town landfill."

Top Caymanian Dishes To Try

CAYMAN-STYLE BEEF

The most tender meat you will ever taste, Cayman-style beef, or "stew beef," is slow-cooked shreds of meat tossed with mouth-watering hot spices and left for hours on end to soak up the divine, flavorsome juices. Traditionally served around Christmas time, it's a winner all year round in our books.

FRIED SNAPPER

Fried fish, usually mahimahi, grouper, or snapper, originates from Cayman's seafaring past. Fillets are marinated in lime, salt, and pepper and fried with onions, peppers, butter, and spices for a delicious traditional dish.

JERK CHICKEN

If you're craving some juicy meat with a fiery kick, you won't be disappointed. Native to Jamaica, this spicy dish, made with scotch bonnet peppers and allspice, is probably the most famous of the Caribbean foods. Smoldering jerk stands are scattered across the island wafting their spicy aromas; follow your nose and you'll easily get your jerk fill. Try pork, a spicy rack of ribs, or the classic chicken.

TURTLE STEW

Perhaps the most traditional meal in the Cayman Islands, turtle stew 9crammed with spices, cassava, potatoes, onions, and peppers) is a firm favorite among locals. All turtle meat on the island comes from the Cayman Islands Turtle Center.

CASSAVA CAKE

A root vegetable, cassava is native to Central and South America but popular all over the tropics. Made with coconut milk, sugar, and spices, cassava cake (or heavy cake) is considered a traditional Caymanian dish. Get a mouthful of the good stuff at Grand Old House in South Sound.

Jerk chicken

COCONUT RUNDOWN

A coconut concoction of mahimahi fish, vegetables, and spice, this dish errs on the side of comfort, and is always a winner on the menu. It's best served with rice and beans as well as plantains on the side—our favorite is at Peppers on West Bay Road.

CARIBBEAN LOBSTER

Caymanians know how to do gourmet—and Caribbean lobster is a great example. Spiny lobster found in the warm waters of the Caribbean is a delicacy and arguably, the best of its kind. You'll find succulent, irresistible lobster dishes in risottos, pastas, and even patties dotted across the island, but you must try the Cayman-style lobster tails from Deckers on Seven Mile Beach. Cooked with hot sauce and scotch bonnet peppers, this spicy, tender dish is nothing short of exquisite.

FISH TEA

Similar to rundown but more a soup than a thick stew, this watery combination is made with fish, onions, peppers, salt, and pepper. It's popular as an evening dish or snack before winding down for the evening. Some locals like to make it from boiled fish heads. Find it at any fish fry or road-side shack across the island.

CONCH STEW

This delicious must-try dish swims with spicy scotch bonnet, conch (a type of sea snail), peppers, coconut milk with a splash of lime and seasoning.

Grand Cayman's Best Beaches

SMITH'S COVE

The quiet little bay in South Sound, Smith Cove is famous for its crystal-clear visibility and out-of-this-world snorkelling. Relax under a giant seagrape tree, jump into the cool water off the rocks, or simply explore.

STARFISH BEACH

This remote, hideaway beach on the northern coast attracts wild starfish to its gentle, turtle grass–lined shores. Wade in the emerald green, deliciously warm waters, watch the sun dip into the ocean, or simply enjoy the castaway experience.

CEMETERY BEACH

With possibly the most powdery white sand on the island, Cemetery Beach, which sits at the northern end of Seven Mile Beach, is a seemingly endless stretch of paradise. The water is crystal clear, great for snorkeling, kayaking, and cooling off.

BAREFOOT BEACH

Barefoot beach is a secluded, narrow stretch of shoreline in Bodden Town with a charming tiki beach hut and alluring waters filled with marine life. A top local spot, this beach has a parking area out front, where you can take a snap or find a shady spot under one of the swaying palms.

RUM POINT BEACH

Famous for its postcard-perfect jetty that slices across its glasslike waters, tranquil Rum Point offers soft, powder-white sand, transparent, shallow waters, and shady hammocks, perfect for lazing. A favorite spot for locals and tourists, it's a popular destination for a leisurely Sunday drive and to watch the fishing boats come in while you sip a chocolatey, boozy mudslide.

Rum Pointe Beach

SEVEN MILE BEACH

This is not only the most popular beach in the Cayman Islands but often ranked among the top in the world. Dotted with luxurious resorts and gourmet restaurants, it offers uninterrupted views and is perfect for snorkelling, jet skiing, sunbathing, or just relaxing.

GOVERNOR'S BEACH

Along West Bay Road you'll find one of the most beautiful beaches on the island. This long, curved stretch is known for its warm sand, shallow water, and drooping casuarina trees that guard its pristine shoreline.

PUBLIC BEACH

With shimmering white sand and strips of blue hues stretching out to the horizon, the views from Public Beach will leave you in awe. Spend a day here playing volleyball, indulging at nearby restaurants, or resting your limbs in a shady spot under a cabana.

SURFER'S BEACH

Postcard-perfect palm trees greet you here, but what truly makes it special are the waves that draw local surfers and bodyboarders.

WEST BAY PUBLIC BEACH

With a backdrop of upscale, high-end resorts to your left, and parking and picnic areas available, this is a great choice for a day spent doing nothing but beach-bumming.

What to Buy

LOCAL ART FROM PURE ART

Decorate your walls with colorful Caymanian art from Pure Art gallery and gifts on South Church Street. Looking for an abstract piece or an intricate oil on canvas for your living room? This quaint little cottage has it all.

BEACH BUBBLES SOAP

For a sweet-smelling souvenir that everyone back home will love, Beach Bubbles Soap store is a stop-off you should have on your itinerary. These deliciously smelling handcrafted tropical soaps and other healing products are made from the old-world neem tree and are popular with locals for their healing medicinal properties.

TORTUGA RUM CAKE

The taste of the Caribbean and a treat you'll want to bring back with you, Tortuga Rum Cakes have been savored by locals and visitors for years. The number one export of the island, it's one of the most popular souvenirs visitors can take home. Moist and airy like a pound cake, but topped with chopped pecans and soaked in rum, the "golden original" flavor has been supplemented by chocolate, pineapple, or Key lime. The main cake factory is on North South Road.

LOCAL POTTERY AND GIFTS

Three Girls and a Kiln Grand Cayman is a group of artists who create intricate local Cayman art. Specializing in ceramics, local crafts, and Cayman creativity, the store in Camana Bay is one not to miss. You can find anything from fun ceramic coasters, Christmas ornaments, and mugs to locally inspired tea towels and kitchenware.

DUTY-FREE PERFUME AND JEWELRY

Grand Cayman is home to a slew of duty-free shops with the latest beauty products, perfume, and jewelry from the world's best brands. From Cartier to Rolex and everything in between, just make sure you bring your wallet (and know what the prices are like back home to ensure you get a good bargain).

Cayman pepper jelly

CAYMAN PEPPER JELLY

What started as a hobby for islander Carol Hay has now become a "must have" in Cayman households and a perfect souvenir gift. Made from locally grown, spicy scotch bonnet peppers, it's a delicious blend of hot and sweet, with a kick is unbeatable and definitely one for the pantry back home. Local tip: it's best served with cream cheese and crackers.

HOT SAUCE

New on the culinary scene, "Fiyah" hot sauce by local chef Thomas Tennant has already become hit in Cayman. There's no denying it brings the heat and has a ton of flavor. The bottled sauces range in heat and seasoning and will give your dish a little Cayman kick.

Kids and Families

Grand Cayman and, to a much lesser extent, the Sister Islands are buzzing with activities and attractions that will keep children of all ages (and their parents) happily occupied. Some resorts and hotels welcome children, others do not, and still others restrict kids to off-season visits. All but the fanciest (and most expensive) restaurants are kid-friendly.

FAMILY-FRIENDLY RESORTS

The **Ritz-Carlton,** one of the most fashionable of the island's resorts, welcomes children at any time with "edu-tainment" programs for all ages, including Jean-Michel Cousteau's Ambassadors of the Environment initiative intro-ducing Cayman's culture and ecology. Less pricey is **Grand Cayman Marriott Beach Resort** on Seven Mile Beach, which has children's programs. Many of the condo complexes toward the northern end of Seven Mile Beach, such as **Christopher Columbus** and **Discovery Point Club,** offer good value and a wide rock-free strand. On Cayman Brac, the **Brac Reef Beach Resort** is best equipped for families. Little Cayman is too quiet for most kids, but the **Little Cayman Beach Resort** can keep children occupied while their parents dive. The **Kimpton Seafire Resort** also offers Camp Seafire for kids, featuring thoughtfully planned programs for ages 3½ to 12, with a creative new theme every day. For smaller children or families who want childcare in their guestrooms, Camp Seafire also offers a nanny service.

FAMILY-FRIENDLY DINING AND ACTIVITIES

Dining out with the family is not an issue, as Grand Cayman has more restaurants than you can count serving a virtual United Nations of cuisines. The Sister Islands are much more limited in their offerings, though the friendly locals will do their utmost to please finicky palates. **Camana Bay** is definitely family-friendly, from climbing the Observation Tower to see gorgeous panoramas, to splashing in the fountains and watching the frequent street performers. Most of the islands' water-based activi-ties cater to kids, including the **Atlantis semisubmersible, Stingray City snorkeling tours,** and the **Dolphin Discovery.** The attractions at the **Cayman Turtle Centre,** including the predator reef and breeding facility, mes-merize all ages, as will learning about blue iguanas at their habitat in the **Queen Elizabeth II Botanical Garden.** Pipes, ramps, and rails galore, not to mention a wave-surf machine at **Black Pearl Skate & Surf Park,** appeal to both kids and adults.

TRAVEL SMART

Updated by
Monica Walton

★ **CAPITAL:**
George Town

POPULATION:
65,722

LANGUAGE:
English

$ CURRENCY:
Cayman Islands dollar

COUNTRY CODE:
1 345

⚠ **EMERGENCIES:**
911

🚗 **DRIVING:**
On the left

⚡ **ELECTRICITY:**
120v/60 cycles; plugs
are U.S. standard
two- and three-prong

🕙 **TIME:**
One hour earlier than
New York during
daylight saving; same
time as New York
otherwise

✈ **AIRPORTS:**
Grand Cayman
(Owen Roberts
International Airport;
GCM); Cayman
Brac (Captain
Charles Kirkconnell
International Airport;
CYB); Little Cayman
(Edward Bodden
Airfield; LYB)

🌐 **WEBSITES**
www.visitcayman-
island.com

CAYMAN
BRAC

LITTLE
CAYMAN

West End

Blossom
Village

Caribbean Sea

West Bay   Old Man
              Bay   Colliers
         GRAND
         CAYMAN

George
Town   Bodden Town

Know Before You Go

COVID-19 has changed the way we travel, and it's likely to continue having an impact well into 2021. A phased border opening with stringent testing, vaccination, and quarantine requirements is likely to continue in the Cayman Islands for the foreseeable future; tourism began to slowly reopen in March 2021.

STORES AND SUPERMARKETS ARE CLOSED ON SUNDAY

The Cayman Islands remains a very religious society. Some restaurants stay open on Sunday, but grocery stores and shops are closed, so tourist have to plan accordingly. Bars and clubs shut their doors at midnight on Saturday night due to the religious beliefs of the locals that Sunday is a day of rest.

DRIVE ON THE LEFT SIDE IN GRAND CAYMAN

Cayman is a British Overseas Territory, and driving is on the left side of the road here, just as in the United Kingdom (even though most cars are imported from the U.S. and Europe and have their steering wheels on the left in the American and European style. Be sure to look the right way when crossing the street, and drive slowly and carefully to start. Drivers tend to adjust quickly, but they still have to pay attention.

NO DRIVING PERMIT NEEDED

Driver's licensing laws continue to evolve in the Cayman Islands, but visitors can now drive using their foreign license without purchasing a separate local driving permit as long as your home license is valid and you have insurance (bring proof that it's valid outside of your home country, or purchase extra insurance along with your car rental). Visitors who have a full, valid driver's license from the United States or Canada can drive for six months in Cayman.

U.S. VISITORS WON'T NEED A POWER ADAPTER

The Cayman Islands uses the same 120-volt standard that is used in the U.S.A. If you're from the United States, you can bring your power units from home to charge laptops, tablets, and mobile phones, and you can use your U.S.-made hair dryer and curling iron. Travelers with other types of power plugs should bring a converter plug to charge all necessary gadgets and may need to bring travel versions of their other appliances if they don't operate on 120 volts.

DRESS FOR WARM WEATHER

The Cayman Islands weather is flip-flop weather year-round, but during rainy season it does get a little wet. Bring rain gear just in case if you're traveling during those months; otherwise, tank tops, shorts, and light T-shirts will work during the day. During July, it's typically around 100°F/37°C, and January often sees weather that's a still-warm 70°F/21°C. But if you are eating inside, the A/C can be cooler, and you may have to dress accordingly.

MAINTAIN THE NORMS

In terms of dress code, swimsuits are fine on the beach or cruise ship, but more formal dress is expected around town (men should always wear a shirt and women a cover-up at the very least) and in your hotel, and at night people dress up a bit more. Men will need to upgrade to a collared shirt and perhaps some long pants if they are eating out, but there are no places where you'll have to dress up.

IT'S EASY TO GET AROUND THE ISLAND BY BUS

If you are staying in Seven Mile Beach, where restaurants may be within walking distance, you may not need to rent a car for your entire visit. It's just $2.50 to ride the bus to popular spots like Rum Point and West Bay. Signs along the main road will guide you where to wait for a minibus; they operate continuously about every 15 minutes from 6 am to early evening, but if you are going out to dinner, you'll probably need to drive or take a taxi. Many tour operators will pick you up at your hotel and bring you back so you won't need to navigate.

THE CAYMAN ISLANDS USES TWO CURRENCIES

CI (Cayman Island dollars) and U.S. dollars are both accepted by everyone here. You'll find that the CI dollar is roughly 20% higher than the U.S. dollar, but all ATMs dispense money in both currencies, and you can choose the one you get. Although the rate doesn't usually change dramatically or suddenly, the Cayman Islands dollar to U.S. dollar exchange rate can fluctuate, so be sure to check what the current exchange rate is before you go.

HURRICANE SEASON IS LONG

Hurricane season lasts officially from June 1 to November 30, roughly half the year. That doesn't mean things shut down entirely, but some businesses close in the summer and reopen again in November, and if resorts close for refurbishment, it's almost always during the summer.

MIND THE SUN

Don't forget your sunscreen, the Caribbean sun can be unforgiving. Remember to wear sunglasses, drink lots of water, and reapply sunscreen regularly to avoid nasty sunburn or heatstroke. If you are going to the beach, try to avoid the afternoon sun from noon to 3, which is the most likely time you'll be sunburned.

Getting Here

Grand Cayman is a relatively small island, and the longest distance you can travel should take no more than a couple of hours. You can get by on Grand Cayman using a combination of tours and local buses (especially if you are staying in the Seven Mile Beach area), but if you want to explore on your own, it's easier with a rental car. Although driving is on the left, British-style, Grand Cayman's well-paved road system makes independent travel fairly easy, though signage is not always clear. Cayman Brac and Little Cayman are even tinier and can be navigated by bike or moped.

✈ Air

Several carriers offer frequent nonstop or direct flights between North America and Grand Cayman's Owen Roberts Airport. Flying time from New York is about four hours, just over an hour from Miami. Only small STOL propeller aircraft serve Cayman Brac and Little Cayman.

AIRPORTS

Grand Cayman's Owen Roberts Airport (GCM) is a modern facility located in the western, busier section of the island, roughly 2 miles (3 km) east of George Town. The current multimillion-dollar expansion and general upgrade (to meet the projected increase in arrivals over the next two decades) was completed in 2019. The airport is about 15 minutes from hotels situated along Seven Mile Beach, about 30 to 45 minutes from the East End and West Bay lodgings, and 10 minutes from George Town. Cayman Brac's Sir Captain Charles Kirkconnell Airport (CYB) can accommodate smaller jets but is only open from 7 am to 7 pm; while Little Cayman's Edward Bodden Airstrip is on the southwest side of the island and can only accommodate prop aircraft due to runway limitations.

GROUND TRANSPORTATION

In Grand Cayman, ground transportation is available immediately outside the customs area of the airport. Taxis aren't metered, but fares are government-regulated (about $15–$30 to resorts along Seven Mile Beach, $60 to the East End). Be sure, however, to confirm the fare before getting into the taxi and whether the price quoted is in U.S. or Cayman dollars.

Round-trip airport transfers are generally included (or at least offered) by hotels on the Sister Islands, where most accommodations sit within 10 minutes' drive of the airports.

Taxis are always available at Grand Cayman's airport. They

don't dependably meet flights on the Sister Islands, so make sure your resort or villa company has made arrangements.

FLIGHTS

All nonstop and direct air service is to Grand Cayman (the country's flag carrier), with connecting flights to Cayman Brac and Little Cayman on a small propeller plane. Some flights only operate in high season. Cayman Airways offers nonstops from several destinations, including Chicago, Dallas, Miami, New York–JFK, and Tampa. American offers service from Miami and Charlotte. Delta flies from Detroit, Minneapolis, and New York–JFK, and from its Atlanta hub. JetBlue flies from JFK and seasonally from Boston. United flies from Washington Dulles and Newark, and Houston. Cayman Airways also flies to both Cayman Brac and Little Cayman. Canadian carrier WestJet flies from Toronto. There's also regularly scheduled flights and also interlsland charter service on Island Air.

 Bicycle

When renting bicycle (or a motor scooter), remember to drive on the left and wear sunblock and a helmet. Bicycles ($15 a day) and scooters ($50 a day) can be rented in George

Town when cruise ships are in port. On Cayman Brac or Little Cayman your hotel can make arrangements for you (most offer complimentary bicycles for local sightseeing). There are two scooter companies on Little Cayman.

Bus

On Grand Cayman, bus service is efficient, inexpensive, and plentiful, running roughly every 15 minutes from 6 am to early evening (though there are no specific timetables). Minivans marked "Omni Bus" are mostly independently operated (there are roughly 40 buses and 24 owners) and run from 6 am to 11 pm (until midnight Friday and Saturday) from West Bay to Rum Point and the East End; service on Sunday is limited. All routes branch from the George Town terminal adjacent to the library on Edward Street and are described in the phone book; color codes denote the nine routes. The one-way fare from George Town to West Bay via Seven Mile Beach is US$2 (covering most popular destinations), to East End destinations US$5, and from West Bay and northern Seven Mile Beach to East End US$3.50 (you pay the driver as you get off). Some bus stops are well marked; others are flexible. Respond

Getting Here

to an approaching bus with a wave; then the driver toots his horn to acknowledge that he has seen you.

Car

Driving is easy on Grand Cayman, albeit on the left. Traffic on the road from Seven Mile Beach to George Town then onto Bodden Town in Grand Cayman is terrible, especially during the 7 to 9 am and 4:30 to 6:30 pm commuting periods. One major coastal highway circumnavigates most of the island (one shortcut bisects the extensive East Districts), though you can get lost in the tangle of side roads in primarily residential West Bay. Exploring Cayman Brac on a scooter is fun and straightforward. You won't really need a car on Little Cayman, though there are a limited number of jeeps for rent; bikes are the preferred mode of transport.

CAR RENTALS

To rent a car in the Cayman Islands, you must have a valid driver's license and major credit card; you do not have to buy a separate local driving permit. Some companies set a minimum age of 25; drivers over 70 may need a certified doctor's note indicating a continuing ability to drive safely. Several dozen agencies rent cars, 4WD vehicles, and SUVs; rates are expensive—ranging from $45 to $95 per day (or $250 to $600 or more per week) in high season. Many firms offer significant discounts in low season, as well as reduced three-day rates. The rental generally includes insurance, pickup and delivery service (or shuttle service to your hotel or the airport), maps, 24-hour emergency service, and unlimited mileage. Car seats are usually available upon request.

The major agencies have offices to the left as you depart from the airport terminal in Grand Cayman; Andy's (a local, family-owned company) is to the right. All require that you walk outdoors for a hundred yards. Make sure your luggage is portable, because there's no shuttle. Many car-rental firms have free pickup and drop-off along Seven Mile Beach (or second branches) so you can rent just on the days you want to tour. Andy's has an office in East End; Cayman Auto Rentals, another local company, only has a location in George Town. Consider security when renting a jeep that cannot be locked. "Midsize" cars here often mean subcompact.

On Cayman Brac, the car-rental companies usually offer free pickup and drop-off at the airport and almost anywhere else if you don't rent your car on arrival or return it before you are ready to leave. All the companies are locally owned.

On Little Cayman you only have one option for car rentals, whether you rent for the day or the week.

CAR INSURANCE

If you own a car, your personal auto insurance may cover a rental to some degree, though not all policies protect you abroad; always read your policy's fine print. If you don't have auto insurance, consider buying the collision- or loss-damage waiver (CDW or LDW) from the car-rental company, which eliminates your liability for damage to the car.

Some credit cards offer CDW coverage, but it's usually supplemental to your own insurance and rarely covers SUVs, minivans, luxury models, and the like. If your coverage is secondary, you may still be liable for loss-of-use costs from the car-rental company. But no credit-card insurance is valid unless you use that card for *all* transactions, from reserving to paying the final bill. All companies exclude car rental in some countries, so be sure to find out about the destination to which you are traveling.

GASOLINE

In Grand Cayman, you can find gasoline stations in and around George Town, the airport, and Seven Mile Beach; a few remain open 24 hours a day. There are two gasoline stations on Cayman Brac and one on Little Cayman. Prices are exorbitant, even compared to those in the United States and most of the Caribbean, especially on the Sister Islands.

PARKING

Park only in approved parking areas. Most hotels offer free parking. Many airports, Camana Bay, George Town, and Seven Mile Beach parking lots are free, but increasing development has prompted some major shopping centers to charge a fee if you park for more than 15 minutes (about $2.50 per hour); however, if you purchase something, parking should be validated and free. There is limited street parking, but watch for signs indicating private parking (in lots as well). Private enforcement companies are employed to discourage interlopers, placing a boot on the wheel and charging CI$75 for removal.

ROAD CONDITIONS

Grand Cayman has well-paved roads that follow the coastline. A network of main highways and bypasses facilitates traffic flow into and out of George

Getting Here

Town. Small signs tacked to trees and poles at intersections point the way to most attractions, and local people are helpful if you get lost. Remote roads are in good repair, yet lighting can be poor at night—and night falls quickly at about 6 pm year-round.

Cayman Brac has one major road that skirts the coast, with a shortcut (Ashton Reid Drive) climbing the Bluff roughly bisecting the island. Little Cayman also provides a coastal route; unpaved sections in less-trammeled areas can become almost impassable after heavy rain. Other than that, goats, chickens, cattle, and the occasional iguana have the right of way.

ROADSIDE EMERGENCIES

Each car-rental agency has a different emergency-assistance provider. In the event of theft, accidents, or breakdowns, call your car-rental agency and follow instructions.

RULES OF THE ROAD

Be mindful of pedestrians and, in the countryside, occasional livestock walking on the road. When someone flashes headlights at you at an intersection, it means "after you." Be especially careful negotiating roundabouts (traffic circles). Observe the speed limit, which is conservative: 30 mph (50 kph) in the country, 20 mph

(30 kph) in town. George Town actually has rush hours: 7 to 9 am and 4:30 to 6:30 pm. Park only in approved parking areas. Always wear your seat belts—it's the law!

Taxi

On Grand Cayman, taxis operate 24 hours a day, but if you anticipate a late night, make pickup arrangements in advance. You can generally not hail one on the street, but you can call for one. Taxis carry up to three passengers for the same price. Fares are set by the government, and they're not cheap, so ask ahead. The tariff increases with the number of riders and bags. Luxury limo service sare also available. Most taxi drivers will take you on an island tour at an hourly rate of about $25 for up to three people. Be sure to settle the price before you start off and agree on whether it's quoted in U.S. or Cayman dollars.

Taxis are scarcer on the Sister Islands; rates are also fixed and fairly prohibitive. Your hotel will provide recommended drivers.

Essentials

🏃 Activities

Although most activities on Grand Cayman are aquatic in nature, landlubbers can do more than just loll on the lovely beaches. There are nature hikes, bird-watching treks, and horseback rides through the island's wilder, more remote areas. The golf scene is well above par for so small an island, with courses designed by Jack "The Golden Bear" Nicklaus and, fittingly, "The White Shark" Greg Norman. Even the most seasoned sea salts might enjoy terra firma, at least for half a day.

BIKING

Mountain bikers will be disappointed by pancake-flat Grand Cayman, but cyclists looking to feel the burn while traversing varied scenery will be pleasantly surprised. The island's extremes, West Bay and East End, are most conducive to letting it fly.

BIRD-WATCHING

The Cayman Islands are an ornithologist's dream, providing perches for a wide range of resident and migratory birds—219 species at last count, many of them endangered, such as the Cayman parrot. The National Trust organizes regular bird-watching field trips conducted by local ornithologists through the Governor Michael Gore Bird Sanctuary, Queen Elizabeth II Botanic Park, Mastic Reserve, Salina Reserve, Central Mangrove Wetland, Meagre Bay Pond Reserve in Pease Bay, Colliers Pond in East End, and Palmetto Pond at Barkers in West Bay. Prime time for bird-watching is either early in the morning or late in the afternoon; take strong binoculars and a field guide to identify the birds.

DIVING

One of the world's leading dive destinations, Grand Cayman has dramatic underwater topography that features plunging walls, soaring skyscraper pinnacles, grottoes, arches, swim-throughs adorned with vibrant sponges, coral-encrusted caverns, and canyons patrolled by lilliputian grunts to gargantuan groupers, darting jacks to jewfish, moray eels to eagle rays. Gorgonians and sea fans wave like come-hither courtesans. Pyrotechnic reefs provide homes for all manner of marine life, ecosystems encased within each other like an intricate series of Chinese boxes.

Reef Watch. This progressive program, a partnership between the Department of the Environment and Cayman Islands Tourism Association, debuted in 1997 during Earth

Essentials

Day activities. The DOE designed a field survey to involve diving and snorkeling tourists in counting and cataloging marine life. To date, more than 1,000 surveys have been completed, helping to estimate species' populations and travel patterns based on sightings and their distance from buoys and other markers, as well as gauging how often equipment touches the fragile reefs. Though not scientifically sound, it does enhance awareness through interaction.

DIVE SITES

There are more than 200 near-pristine dive sites, many less than a half mile from the island and easily accessible, including wreck, wall, and shore options. Add exceptional visibility from 80 to 150 feet (no rivers deposit silt) and calm, current-free water at a constant bathlike 80°F. Cayman is serious about conservation, with stringently enforced laws to protect the fragile, endangered marine environment (fines up to $500,000 and a year in prison for damaging living coral, which can take years to regrow), protected by the creation of Marine Park, Replenishment, and Environmental Park Zones. Local water-sports operators enthusiastically cooperate: most boats use biodegradable cleansers and environmentally friendly drinking cups. Moorings at all popular dive sites prevent coral and sponge damage due to continual anchoring; in addition, diving with gloves is prohibited to reduce the temptation to touch.

Pristine water, breathtaking coral formations, and plentiful marine life including hammerheads and hawksbill turtles mark the **North Wall**—a world-renowned dive area along the North Side of Grand Cayman.

Trinity Caves in West Bay is a deep dive with numerous canyons starting at about 60 feet and sloping to the wall at 130 feet. The South Side is the deepest, with the top of its wall starting 80-feet deep before plummeting, though its shallows offer a lovely labyrinth of caverns and tunnels in such sites as **Japanese Gardens** and **Della's Delight.**

The less-visited, virgin East End is less varied geographically beyond the magnificent **Ironshore Caves** and **Babylon Hanging Gardens** (trees of black coral plunging 100 feet), but it teems with "Swiss-cheese" swim-throughs and exotic life in such renowned gathering spots as **The Maze** (a hangout for reef, burse, and occasional hammerhead sharks), **Snapper Hole,** and **Grouper Grotto.**

The Cayman Islands government acquired the 251-foot, decommissioned USS *Kittiwake* (⊕ *www.kittiwake-cayman.com*). Sunk in January 2011, it has already become an exciting new dive attraction, while providing necessary relief for some of the most frequently visited dive sites. The top of the bridge is just 15 feet down, making it accessible to snorkelers. There's a single-use entry fee of $10 ($5 for snorkelers).

The **Cayman Dive 365** (⊕ *www.dive365cayman.com*) initiative is part of a commitment to protect reefs from environmental overuse. New dive sites will be introduced while certain existing sites are "retired" to be rested and refreshed. Visitors are encouraged to sponsor and name a new dive site from the list of selected coordinates.

SHORE DIVING

Shore diving around the island provides easy access to kaleidoscopic reefs, fanciful rock formations, and enthralling shipwrecks. The areas are well marked by buoys to facilitate navigation. If the water looks rough where you are, there's usually a side of the island that's wonderfully calm.

DIVE OPERATORS

As one of the Caribbean's top diving destinations, Grand Cayman is blessed with many top-notch dive operations offering diving, instruction, and equipment for sale and rent. A single-tank boat dive averages $80, a two-tank dive $105–$129 (with discounts for multi-day packages). Snorkel-equipment rental is about $15 a day. Divers are required to be certified and possess a "C" card. If you're getting certified, to save time during your limited holiday you can start the book and pool work at home and finish the open-water portion in warm, clear Cayman waters. Certifying agencies offer this referral service all around the world.

When choosing a dive operator, ask if they require that you stay with the group, and whether they provide towels, camera rinse water, protection from inclement weather, tank-change service, beach or resort pickup, and/or snacks between dives. Ask what dive options they have during a winter storm (called a nor'wester here), as well as what kind of boat they use. Don't assume that a small, less-crowded boat is better. Some large boats are more comfortable, even when full, than a tiny, uncovered boat without a marine toilet. Small boats, however, offer more personal service and less-crowded dives.

Essentials

Strict marine protection laws prohibit you from taking any marine life from many areas around the island. Always check with the **Department of Environment** (*345/949–8469*) before diving, snorkeling, and fishing. To report violations, call **Marine Enforcement** (*345/948–6002*).

FISHING

The Cayman Islands are widely hailed as a prime action-packed destination for all types of sportfishing, from casting in the flats for the wily, surprisingly strong "gray ghost" bonefish, to trolling for giant, equally combative blue marlin. Conditions are ideal for big game fish: the water temperature varies only 8 to 10 degrees annually, so the bait and their pelagic predators hang out all year. The big lure for anglers is the big game-fish run near the coast, as close as a quarter-mile offshore.

Experienced, knowledgeable local captains charter boats with top-of-the-line equipment, bait, ice, and often lunch included in the price (usually $550–$750 per half day, $900–$1,500 for a full day). Options include deep-sea, reef, bone, tarpon, light-tackle, and fly-fishing. June and July are particularly good all-around months for reeling in blue marlin, yellow- and blackfin tuna, dolphinfish (dorado), and bonefish. Bonefish have a second season in the winter months, along with wahoo and skipjack tuna. Marine Park laws prohibit fishing or taking any type of marine life in protected areas. Local captains promote conservation and sportsmanship through catch-and-release of both reef and pelagic fish not intended for eating and all billfish, unless they are local records or potential tournament winners.

SAILING

Though Cayman has a large sailing community, it isn't a big charter-yacht destination. Still, you can skipper your own craft (albeit sometimes under the watchful eye of the boat's captain). The protected waters of the North Sound are especially delightful, but chartering a sailboat is also a wonderful way to discover lesser-known snorkeling, diving, and fishing spots around the island.

SEA EXCURSIONS

The most impressive sights in the Cayman Islands are on and under water, and several submarines, semisubmersibles, glass-bottom boats, and Jules Verne–like contraptions allow you to see these underwater wonders without getting your feet wet. Sunset sails, dinner cruises, and other theme (dance, booze, pirate) cruises are available from $35 to $90 per person.

SNORKELING

The proximity of healthy, Technicolor reef to the Grand Cayman shore means endless possibilities for snorkelers. Some sites require you to simply wade or swim into the surf; others are only accessible via boat. Nearly every snorkeling outfit follows the same route, beginning with the scintillating Stingray City and Sandbar. They usually continue to the adjacent Coral Gardens and often farther out along the Barrier Reef. Equipment is included, sometimes drinks, snacks, and lunch. Half-day tours run $35–$40, full-day $60–$75, and there are often extras such as kids' discounts and a complimentary shuttle to and from Seven Mile Beach resorts. Other popular trips combine Eden Rock, Cheeseburger Reef, and the wreck of the *Cali* off George Town. Most decent-size boats offer cover, but bring sunscreen and a hat.

SNORKELING SITES

Barrier Reef. Separating the North Sound and Cayman's celebrated wall drop-off (part of a 6,000-foot underwater mountain), this reef has snorkeling along its shallow side, which is crawling with critters of all shapes, sizes, and colors.

Cemetery Reef. Sitting 50 yards out from the north end of Seven Mile Beach, within walking distance of several condo resorts, this reef has fish that are accustomed to being fed. Blue tangs, blue-headed wrasse, bat jacks, and black durgeon could swarm around you.

Cheeseburger Reef. This reef earned its unusual moniker thanks to its location straight out from the downtown Burger King. It's also known as Soto's Reef after legendary diver Bob Soto, one of the islands' original dive operators. The eye-popping, 12,000-year-old coral formations begin 20 yards offshore, with larger heads a mere 10 feet down, though it reaches depths of 40 feet. You can swim through numerous tunnels where turtles and tarpon hang out; people have long fed fish in the area, but beware of snapping snappers if you bring food.

Coral Gardens. Near Stingray Sandbar, this snorkeling site attracts nurse sharks, moray eels, queen conch, lobster, and schools of jacks, tangs, sergeant majors, parrot fish, yellowtails, and others playing hide-and-seek with riotously colored soft and hard corals. It really is like swimming in an aquarium.

Essentials

Eden Rock. Though this site is even more spectacular for divers, who can explore its caves and tunnels, from the surface you can still see schools of sergeant majors, yellowtail snappers, parrot fish, tarpon, Bermuda chubs, even the occasional stingray and turtle.

Stingray City Sandbar. This site (as opposed to Stingray City, a popular 12-foot dive) is the island's stellar snorkeling attraction. Dozens of boats head here several times daily. It's less crowded on days with fewer cruise ships in port.

Wreck of the *Cali.* You can still identify the engines and winches of this old sailing freighter, which settled about 20 feet down. The sponges are particularly vivid, and tropical fish, shrimp, and lobster abound. Many operators based in George Town and Seven Mile Beach come here.

SQUASH AND TENNIS

Most resorts and condominium complexes have their own courts, often lighted for night play, but guests have top priority. When empty, you can book a court, which normally costs around $25 per hour.

WINDSURFING

The East End's reef-protected shallows extend for miles, offering ideal blustery conditions (15 to 35 mph in winter, 6- to 10-knot southerlies in summer) for windsurfing and kiteboarding. Boarders claim only rank amateurs will "tea-bag" (kite-speak for skidding in and out of the water) in those "nuking" winds. They also rarely "Hindenburg" (stall due to lack of breeze) off West Bay's Palmetto Point and Conch Point.

Dining

Obviously seafood reigns supreme in the Cayman Islands, where it's served everywhere from tiny family-run shanties to decadently decorated bistros. But befitting Grand Cayman's reputation as a sophisticated, multinational destination (with residents from 120 countries at last count), you can find a smorgasbord of savory options from terrific Tex-Mex to Thai to Italian. Menus could highlight by-the-book bouillabaisse or barbecue, kebabs or cannelloni, ceviche, or sushi. This is one destination where larger resorts generally have excellent restaurants. Two must-try local delicacies are conch, particularly fritters and chowder, and turtle (protected but farmed); the latter is stewed or served like a steak. Many restaurants offer kids' menus, and vegetarians should find acceptable options.

Today, despite its small size, comparative isolation, and British colonial trappings, Grand Cayman offers a smorgasbord of gastronomic goodies. With more than 100 eateries, something should suit and sate every palate and pocketbook (especially once you factor in fast-food franchises sweeping the islandscape like tumbleweed and stalls dispensing local specialties).

The term *melting pot* describes both the majority of menus and the multicultural population. It's not uncommon to find "American" dishes at an otherwise Caribbean restaurant, Indian fare at an Italian eatery (and vice versa). The sheer range of dining options from Middle Eastern to Mexican reflects the island's cosmopolitan, discriminating clientele. Imported ingredients reflect the United Nations, with chefs sourcing salmon from Norway, foie gras from Périgord, and lamb from New Zealand. Wine lists can be equally global in scope (often receiving awards from such oeno-bibles as *Wine Spectator*). Don't be surprised to find both Czech and Chilean staffers at a remote East End restaurant.

MEALS AND MEALTIMES

Most restaurants serve breakfast from 7 to 10 am, lunch from noon to 3 pm, and dinner from 6 to 11 pm. But these hours can vary widely, especially at remote resorts on Grand Cayman's East End and West Bay, as well as on the Sister Islands, which have few independent eateries. Every strip mall along Grand Cayman's Seven Mile Beach has at least one restaurant open late (often doubling as a lounge or nightclub); many beachfront bars also offer late dining, especially on weekends. Restaurants are likeliest to shutter on Sunday, especially in the less-trafficked areas. Since most grocery stores also close Sunday, prepare for contingencies, especially if you're staying at an individual villa or condo. If you arrive on Saturday, when most villa and condo rentals begin, make sure you do your grocery shopping that afternoon.

Unless otherwise noted, the restaurants listed *in this guide* are open daily for lunch and dinner.

PAYING

Major credit cards are widely accepted, even on the Sister Islands, though some smaller local establishments only accept cash.

Essentials

RESERVATIONS AND DRESS

Grand Cayman is both cosmopolitan and conservative, so scantily clad diners are frowned upon or downright refused seating. Many tonier establishments require long pants and collared shirts for gentlemen in the evening (lunch is generally more casual). Footwear and something to cover bathing suits (a sarong or sundress for women, T-shirt and shorts for men) are required save at some beachfront bars. The Sister Islands are far more casual. Reservations are strongly recommended for dinner at most restaurants throughout the islands.

We mention dress only when men are required to wear a jacket or a jacket and tie.

BEER, WINE, AND SPIRITS

Beer, wine, and spirits are readily available at most restaurants. Some pricier restaurants take great pride in their wine lists. Aficionados of local products may want to try the refreshing Caybrew beers (the nutty, smoky dark amber pairs well with many foods), Seven Fathoms rum, and Tortuga rum (the 12-year-old is a marvelous after-dinner sipper in place of Cognac or single-malt Scotch).

PRICES

Since nearly everything must be imported, prices average about 25% higher than those in a major U.S. city. Many restaurants add a 10%–15% service charge to the bill; be sure to check before leaving a tip (waiters usually receive only a small portion of any included gratuities, so leave something extra at your discretion for good service). Alcohol can send your meal tab skyrocketing. Buy liquor duty-free, either at the airport before your flight to the Cayman Islands or in one of the duty-free liquor stores that can be found in almost every strip mall on Grand Cayman, and enjoy a cocktail or nightcap from the comfort of your room or balcony. Cayman customs limits you to two bottles per person. Lunch often offers the same or similar dishes at a considerable discount. Finally, when you are figuring your dining budget, remember that the Cayman dollar is worth 25% more than the U.S. dollar, and virtually all menus are priced in Cayman dollars.

What It Costs in U.S. Dollars			
$	$$	$$$	$$$$
RESTAURANTS			
under $12	$12–$20	$21–$30	over $30

⊕ Health and Safety

Health concerns are minimal in the Cayman Islands, and Grand Cayman offers some of the Caribbean's finest medical facilities. Though there have been isolated cases of dengue fever (one or two annually, contracted elsewhere), the last on-island outbreak was in 2005. The CDC does recommend hepatitis A and typhoid vaccinations to be on the safe side. Airlift to Miami for serious emergencies is available. Physicians are highly qualified and speak English. Be sure to pack prescription medications; consider wearing a MedicAlert ID tag if you suffer from such chronic conditions as diabetes, epilepsy, or heart disease. Though many hospitals offer reciprocity with U.S. insurers, you can also purchase medical-only insurance. Tap water is perfectly safe to drink throughout all three islands. Be sure to wash fruit thoroughly or, better yet, peel it before eating. The subtropic sun can be fierce, especially at midday. Be sure to wear sunglasses and a hat, and use high-SPF sunscreen (most U.S. brands are available). Beware of dehydration and heat stroke; take it easy the first couple of days. Insects can be a real nuisance during the wet season (July–November); bring along repellent to ward off mosquitoes and sand flies. Shops also stock numerous name brands.

COVID-19

A novel coronavirus brought all travel to a virtual standstill in the first half of 2020. Although the illness is mild in most people, some experience severe and even life-threatening complications. Once travel started up again, albeit slowly and cautiously, travelers were asked to be particularly careful about hygiene and to avoid any unnecessary travel, especially if they are sick.

Older adults, especially those over 65, have a greater chance of having severe complications from COVID-19. The same is true for people with weaker immune systems or those living with some types of medical conditions, including diabetes, asthma, heart disease, cancer, HIV/AIDS, kidney disease, and liver disease. Starting two weeks before a trip, anyone planning to travel should be on the lookout for some of the following symptoms: cough, fever, chills, trouble breathing, muscle pain, sore throat, new loss of smell or taste. If you experience any of these symptoms, you should not travel at all.

And to protect yourself during travel, do your best to avoid contact with people showing

Essentials

symptoms. Wash your hands often with soap and water. Limit your time in public places, and, when you are out and about, wear a cloth face mask that covers your nose and mouth. Indeed, a mask may be required in some places, such as on an airplane or in a confined space like a theater, where you share the space with a lot of people. You may wish to bring extra supplies, such as disinfecting wipes, hand sanitizer (12-ounce bottles were allowed in carry-on luggage at this writing), and a first-aid kit with a thermometer.

Given how abruptly travel was curtailed in March 2020, it is wise to consider protecting yourself by purchasing a travel insurance policy that will reimburse you for any costs related to COVID-19 related cancellations. Not all travel insurance policies protect against pandemic-related cancellations, so always read the fine print.

CRIME

Though crime isn't a major problem in the Cayman Islands, take normal precautions. Lock your room, and don't leave valuables—particularly passports, tickets, and wallets—in plain sight or unattended on the beach. Use your hotel safe. Don't carry too much money or flaunt expensive jewelry on the street. For personal safety,

avoid walking on the beach or on unlighted streets at night. Lock your rental car, and don't pick up hitchhikers. Using or trafficking in illegal drugs is strictly prohibited in the Cayman Islands. Any offense is punishable by a hefty fine, imprisonment, or both.

Immunizations

There are no immunization requirements for visitors traveling to the Cayman Islands for tourism.

Lodging

Grand Cayman offers a wide range of lodgings in all price categories (though it ranks as one of the more expensive Caribbean destinations). You'll find luxury resorts, hotels both large and intimate, fully equipped condos, stylish individual villas, B&Bs, and more affordable locally run guesthouses. Quality, professionalism, high-tech conveniences, and service all rank among the region's best. With a few notable exceptions, condo resorts rule Seven Mile Beach (some hotels lie across the coastal "highway"). These are particularly attractive family options, as they include kitchen facilities. Cayman Brac and Little

Cayman accommodations emphasize function above glitz and glamour (though most lack neither character nor characters), befitting the Sister Islands' status as top-notch scuba-diving destinations. Both have villas, condo resorts, and small hotels that often run on an all-inclusive or meal-plan basis and simple, family-run inns.

LODGING OPTIONS
HOTELS AND RESORTS

Grand Cayman offers something for every traveler, with well-known chain properties in every price range and style. Accommodations run the gamut from outrageously deluxe to all-suites to glorified motor lodges. Add to that locally run hostelries that often offer better bang for the buck. Still, in a Caymanian quirk, condo resorts take up most of the prime beach real estate. And, with a couple of exceptions, hotels along Seven Mile Beach actually sit across the road from the beach.

B&BS, INNS, AND GUESTHOUSES

They may be some distance from the beach and short on style and facilities, or they may be surprisingly elegant, but all these lodgings offer a friendly atmosphere, equally friendly prices, and your best shot at getting to know the locals.

Rooms are clean and simple at the very least, and most have private baths.

CONDOMINIUMS AND PRIVATE VILLAS

On Grand Cayman the number of available condos and villas greatly outnumbers hotel rooms. Most condos are very similar, with telephones, satellite TV, air-conditioning, living and dining areas, patios, and parking. Differences are the quality of in-condo amenities, facilities within their individual complexes (though pools, hot tubs, and barbecue grills are usually standard), proximity to town and the beach, and views. Some condos are privately owned and rented out directly by the owners; other complexes are made up solely of short-term rentals.

Grand Cayman's private villa rentals range from cozy one-bedroom bungalows to grand five-bedroom manses. Some stand completely independent; others may be located in a larger complex or enclave. Although at first glance rental fees for villas may seem high, larger units can offer significant savings over hotels for families or couples traveling together. Few hotels on Grand Cayman are so moderately priced. And, as in a condo, a full kitchen helps reduce the stratospheric price

Essentials

of dining out; a laundry room helps with cleanup, especially for families. Unless otherwise noted, all villas have landline phones, and local calls are usually free; phones are generally locked for international calls, though Internet phone service could be included. Villa agents can usually help you rent a cell phone.

Rates are highest during the winter season from mid-December through mid-April. Most condo and villa rentals require a minimum stay, often five to seven nights in high season (during the Christmas holiday season the minimum will be at least one week and is sometimes two weeks, plus there are exorbitant fees). Off-season minimums are usually three to five nights.

Several of the condo- and villa-rental companies have websites where you can see pictures of the privately owned units and villas they represent; many properties are represented exclusively, others handled by several agents. In general, the farther north you go on Seven Mile Beach, the older and more affordable the property. Note also that many offices close on Sunday; if that's your date of arrival, they'll usually make arrangements for your arrival. There's often no maid service on Sunday either, as

the island practically shuts down.

We no longer recommend individual private villas, especially since they frequently change agents. Nevertheless, among the properties we've inspected worth looking for are Coral Reef, Venezia, Villa Habana, Great Escapes, Fishbones, and Pease Bay House.

The **Cayman Islands Department of Tourism** (⊕ *www.cayman-islands.ky*) provides a list of condominiums and small rental apartments. There are several condo and villa enclaves available on the beach, especially on the North Side near Cayman Kai, away from bustling Seven Mile Beach.

Quoted prices for villa and private condo rentals usually include government tax and often service fees (be sure to verify this). As a general rule of thumb, Seven Mile Beach properties receive daily maid service except on Sunday, but at villas and condos elsewhere on the island, extra services such as cleaning must be prearranged for an extra charge.

WHERE SHOULD YOU STAY?

Seven Mile Beach is Boardwalk and Park Place for most vacationers. In a quirk of development, however, most of the hotels sit across the street from the beach (though they usually have beach clubs, bars, water-sports concessions, and other facilities directly on the sand). Most of Grand Cayman's condo resorts offer direct access to Grand Cayman's prime sandy real estate. Snorkelers should note that only the northern and southern ends of SMB feature spectacular reef development; the northern end is much quieter, so if you're looking for action, stay anywhere from the Westin Grand Cayman south, where all manner of restaurants and bars are walkable.

Tranquil **West Bay** retains the feel of an old-time fishing village; diving is magnificent in this area, but lodging options are limited, especially now that the long-promised Mandarin Oriental remains on indefinite hold.

Those who want to get away from it all should head to the bucolic **East End** and **North Side,** dotted with condo resorts and villas. The dive sites here are particularly pristine.

The **Cayman Kai/Rum Point,** starting at West Bay across the North Sound, offers the single largest concentration of villas and condo resorts, stressing barefoot elegance.

LODGING PRICES

Brace yourself for resort prices—there are few accommodations in the lower-cost ranges in Grand Cayman. You'll also find no big all-inclusive resorts on Grand Cayman, and very few offer a meal plan of any kind. Happily, parking is always free at island hotels and resorts.

What It Costs in U.S. Dollars			
$	$$	$$$	$$$$
HOTELS			
under $275	$275–$375	$376–$475	over $475

$ Money

You should not need to change money in Grand Cayman, because U.S. dollars are readily accepted, though you may get some change in Cayman dollars. ATMs accepting MasterCard and Visa with Cirrus affiliation are readily available in George Town; you usually have the option of U.S. or Cayman dollars. The Cayman dollar is pegged to the U.S. dollar at the rate of approximately CI$1 to $1.25, and divided into a hundred cents, with coins of 1¢, 5¢, 10¢, and 25¢ and notes of $1, $5, $10, $25, $50, and $100. There's no $20 bill. Traveler's checks and major credit

Essentials

cards are widely accepted. Be sure you know which currency is being quoted when making a purchase.

CREDIT CARDS

It's a good idea to inform your credit-card company before you travel. Record all your credit-card numbers—as well as the phone numbers to call if your cards are lost or stolen—in a safe place, so you're prepared should something go wrong. Both MasterCard and Visa have general numbers you can call (collect if you're abroad) if your card is lost, but you're better off calling the number of your issuing bank, since MasterCard and Visa usually just transfer you to your bank; your bank's number is usually printed on your card.

If you plan to use your credit card for cash advances, you'll need to apply for a PIN at least two weeks before your trip. Although it's usually cheaper (and safer) to use a credit card abroad for large purchases (so you can cancel payments or be reimbursed if there's a problem), note that some credit-card companies *and* the banks that issue them add substantial percentages to all foreign transactions, whether they're in a foreign currency or not. Check on these fees before leaving home, so there

won't be any surprises when you get the bill.

Nightlife

Despite Grand Cayman's conservatism and small size, the nightlife scene looms surprisingly large, especially on weekends. Choices include boisterous beach-and-brew hangouts, swanky wine bars, pool halls, sports bars, jammed and jamming dance clubs, live entertainment, and cultural events. A smoking ban was instituted in 2010 for night-spots and restaurants (one preexisting cigar bar and a hookah lounge received special dispensation).

Most major resorts, clubs, and bars offer some kind of performance, including lavish rum-and-reggae limbo/fire-eating/stilt-walking extravaganzas. Local bands with a fan(atic) following include soft-rock duo Hi-Tide; the Pandemonium Steelband; reggae-influenced trio Swanky; hard rockers Ratskyn (who've opened for REO Speedwagon, Mötley Crüe, and Bon Jovi); blues/funk purveyors Madamspeaker; and neo-punk rockers the Blow Holes. Other names to look for are Ka, I'Wild Knights, Island Vibes, C.I., Lammie, Heat, Gone Country, and Coco Red.

Consult the "Get Out" section in the Friday edition of the *Caymanian Compass* for listings of live music, movies, theater, and other entertainment. Local magazines such as *Key to Cayman, What's Hot,* and *Destination Cayman* can be picked up free of charge around the island, sometimes providing coupons for discounts and/or freebies. Bars remain open until 1 am, and clubs are generally open from 10 pm until 3 am, but they can't serve liquor after midnight on Saturday and they do not permit dancing on Sunday. Although shorts and sarongs are usually acceptable attire at beachside bars, smart casual defines the dress code for clubbing.

🌐 Passports

All visitors to the Cayman Islands must have a valid passport and a return or ongoing ticket to enter the Cayman Islands. A birth certificate and photo ID are *not* sufficient proof of citizenship.

🎭 Performing Arts

Grand Cayman mounts special events throughout the year. The Cayman National Orchestra performs in disparate venues from the Cracked Conch restaurant to First Baptist Church. There's a burgeoning theater scene. Many new works use religious themes as a launching pad for meditations on issues relevant to current events, such as the Cayman Drama Society (🌐 *caymandramasociety.wildapricot.org/*), *The Judith Code,* updating the biblical heroine's story to a present-day London of TV talk-show hosts and terrorist coalitions; the company also produces stimulating children's fare (*Mort,* based on Terry Pratchett's *Discworld* novels about a young boy apprenticed to Death), as well as escapist crowd-pleasing revivals like *Hairspray* and *Grease.*

🛍 Shopping

There's no sales tax, and there is plenty of duty-free merchandise on Grand Cayman, including jewelry, china, crystal, perfumes, and cameras. Savings on luxury goods range between 10% and 25%. Notable exceptions are liquor, which is available minus that tariff only at specially designated shops, and haute couture (though the ritzier resort shops stock some designer labels). "Brand Cayman" is the local nickname for the glamorous shops along Cardinal Avenue, the local answer to New York's

Essentials

Madison Avenue and Beverly Hills's Rodeo Drive. Esteemed names include Cartier, Waterford, and Wedgwood.

Worthy local items include woven thatch mats and baskets, coconut soap, hardwood carvings, jewelry made from a marblelike stone called Caymanite (from Cayman Brac's cliffs, a striated amalgam of several metals), and authentic sunken treasure often fashioned into jewelry, though the last is never cheap (request a certificate of authenticity if one isn't offered). You'll also find individual artists' ateliers and small, colorful craft shops whose owners often love discussing the old days and traditions. Bear in mind that most major attractions feature extensive and/or intriguing gift shops, whether at the Turtle Centre, National Trust, or the National Gallery.

Local palate pleasers include treats made by the Tortuga Rum Company (both the famed cakes and the actual distilled spirit, including a sublime 12-year-old rum), Cayman Honey, Cayman Taffy, and Cayman Sea Salt (from the ecofriendly "farm" of the same name). Seven Fathoms is the first working distillery actually in Cayman itself, its award-winning rums aged underwater (hence the name). Also seek out such gastronomic goodies as jams, sauces, and vinegars from Hawley Haven and Whistling Duck Farms on the eastern half of the island. Cigar lovers, take note: some shops carry famed Cuban brands, but you must enjoy them on the island; bringing them back to the United States is illegal.

An almost unbroken line of strip malls runs from George Town through Seven Mile Beach, most of them presenting shopping and dining options galore. The ongoing Camana Bay mega-development already glitters with glam shops, including Island Companies' largest and grandest store offering the hautest name-brand jewelry, watches, and duty-free goods.

💲 Taxes

At the airport, each adult passenger leaving Grand Cayman must pay a departure tax of $25 (CI$20), payable in either Caymanian or U.S. currency. It may be included in cruise packages as a component of port charges; it's usually added to airfare—check with your carrier—but if not, must be paid in cash by each traveler prior to entering the secure area of the airport.

A 10% government tax is added to all hotel bills. A 10% service charge is often added to hotel bills and restaurant checks in lieu of a tip, but this is not a government tax. There is no V.A.T. or comparable tariff on goods and services.

💵 Tipping

At large hotels a service charge is generally included and can be anywhere from 6% to 10%; smaller establishments and some villas and condos leave tipping up to you. Although tipping is customary at restaurants, note that some automatically include 10%–15% on the bill—so check the tab carefully. At your discretion, tip another 5% or more to recognize extraordinary service. Taxi drivers expect a 10%–15% tip. Bellmen and porters expect $1 per bag, more in luxury hotels (especially if you bring lots of luggage). Tip the concierge (if your resort has one) anywhere from $10 to $100, depending on services rendered and length of stay. Tips are not expected simply for handing out maps and making the occasional dinner reservation. Spa personnel should receive 15%–20% of the treatment price (but verify that a service fee wasn't already added).

📍 Visitor Information

The Cayman Islands has tourist offices in the United States, where you can get brochures and maps in advance of your trip. There are also tourism offices on the islands for on-site help.

Cayman Islands *Destination* magazine is the local tourist magazine. Cayman Compass is the online version of the national newspaper.

📅 When to Go

High Season: Mid-December through mid-April is the most popular, and most expensive, time to visit. Good hotels book up, so plan ahead.

Low Season: From August to late October, temperatures get hot and the weather muggy, with high risks of tropical storms. Many upscale hotels close for annual renovations or offer deep discounts.

Value Season: From late April to July and again November to mid-December, hotel prices drop 20% to 50% from high-season prices. There are chances of scattered showers, but expect sun-kissed days and fewer crowds.

Contacts

Air

AIRLINES American Airlines.
☎ *345/949–0666* ⊕ *www.
aa.com.* **Cayman Airways.**
☎ *345/949–2311* ⊕ *www.
caymanairways.com.* **Delta.**
☎ *345/945–8430* ⊕ *www.delta.
com.* **Island Air.** ✉ *100 Roberts
Dr., George Town* ☎ *345/949–
5252* ⊕ *www.islandair.ky.*
JetBlue. ☎ *855/710–2951*
⊕ *www.jetblue.com.* **United.**
☎ *800/241–6522* ⊕ *www.unit-
ed.com.* **WestJet.** ☎ *888/937–
8538* ⊕ *www.westjet.com.*

**AIRPORTS Edward Bodden
Airfield (LYB).** ✉ *Guy Banks Rd.,
Blossom Village* ☎ *345/948–
0021* ⊕ *www.caymanairports.
com.* **Owen Roberts International
Airport (GCM).** ✉ *298 Owen
Roberts* ☎ *345/943–7070*
⊕ *www.caymanairports.com.*
**Sir Captain Charles Kirkconnell
International Airport (CYB).**
✉ *Church Cl, West End.*

Bicycle

**RENTAL COMPANIES Scooten!
Scooters!.** ☎ *345/916–4971*
⊕ *www.scootenscooters.com.*

Bus

**CONTACTS Bus Information
Hotline.** ☎ *345/945–5100*
✏ *cayman.transport@gov.ky*
⊕ *thebusschedule.com/EN/ky.*

Car

**GRAND CAYMAN CAR
RENTALS Andy's Rent a Car.**
☎ *345/949–8111, 345/949–8111
toll-free* ⊕ *www.andys.
ky.* **Avis.** ☎ *345/949–2468*
⊕ *www.aviscayman.com.*
Budget. ☎ *345/949–5605*
⊕ *www.budgetcayman.com.*
Cayman Auto Rentals. ✉ *N.
Church St., George Town*
☎ *345/949–1013* ⊕ *www.
caymanautorentals.com.ky.*
Dollar Thrifty. ☎ *345/949–6640,
800/367–2277* ⊕ *www.thrifty.
com.* **Hertz Cayman.** ☎ *800/654–
3131, 345/943–4378 toll-free,
345/943–4378* ⊕ *www.hertz-
cayman.com.*

**CAYMAN BRAC CAR RENTALS
B&S Motor Ventures.** ✛ *Within
walking distance of Cayman
Brac Beach Resort, Brac
Caribbean Beach Villas, and
Carib Sands* ☎ *345/948–1646*
⊕ *www.bandsmv.com.* **CB
Rent-a-Car.** ✉ *West End Rd.*
☎ *345/948–2424* ⊕ *www.
cbrent-a-car.com.* **Four D's Car
Rental.** ✉ *Kidco Bldg., Bert
Marson Dr.* ☎ *345/948–1599,
345/948–0459.*

LITTLE CAYMAN CAR RENT-ALS Little Cayman Car Rental.
✉ 898 Guy Banks Rd., Blossom Village ☎ 345/948–1000 ✉ littl-cay@candw.ky.

🇺🇸 Embassy/Consulate
CONTACTS U.S. Consular Agen-cy. ✉ 202B Smith Rd., Cayman Centre, 150 Smith Rd., George Town ☎ 345/945–8173 ✉ cay-manacs@state.gov.

🛏 Lodging
CONTACTS Cayman Island Vacations. ☎ 813/854–1201, 888/208–8935 ⊕ www.caymanvacation.com. **Cayman Villas.** ✉ 177 Owen Roberts Dr., George Town ☎ 800/235–5888, 345/945–4144 ⊕ www.cay-manvillas.com. **Grand Cayman Villas.** ✉ 846 Frank Sound Rd., George Town ☎ 866/358–8455, 345/946–9524 ⊕ www.grandcaymanvillas.net. **WIMCO.** ☎ 888/997–3970 ⊕ www.wimco.com.

🚖 Taxi
CONTACTS A.A. Transportation Services. ☎ 345/926–8294 ⊕ www.aatransportation.weebly.com. **Charlie's Super Cab.** ✉ Elgin Ave., George Town ☎ 345/926–4748, 345/926–6590 ⊕ www.charliescabs.net.

📍 Visitor Information
CONTACTS Cayman Compass. ☎ 345/949–5111 ⊕ www.caymancompass.com. **Cayman Islands Department of Tourism.** ☎ 212/889–9009 in New York City, 877/422–9626 in U.S., 345/949–0623 in Cayman Islands ⊕ www.visitcayman-islands.com. **Cayman Islands Destination Magazine.** ⊕ www.destination.ky.

Weddings and Honeymoons

Getting married in the Cayman Islands is a breeze, and each year many couples tie the knot here. Most choose to say their vows on lovely Seven Mile Beach, with the sun setting into the azure sea as their picture-perfect backdrop. You can literally leave things up in the air, getting hitched while hovering in a helicopter. A traditional church wedding can even be arranged, after which you trot away to your life together in a horse-drawn carriage.

THE BIG DAY

Choosing the Location. Choose from beaches, bluffs, gardens, private residences, historic buildings, resort lawns, and places of worship for the ceremony or reception. Most couples choose to say their vows on Seven Mile Beach. Underwater weddings in full scuba gear with schools of fish as impromptu witnesses are also possible (kissing with mask on optional); Cathy Church can photograph the undersea event (⇨ *Shopping in Chapter 3*). You can also get hitched while hovering in a helicopter. If you decide to hold the event outdoors, be sure you have a backup plan in case of rain.

Finding a Wedding Planner. The best way to plan your wedding in the Cayman Islands is to contact a wedding coordinator (resorts such as the Wyndham Reef, Westin Grand Cayman, Kimpton Seafire, and Ritz-Carlton have one on staff), who will offer a wide variety of packages to suit every taste and budget. All the logistics and legalities will be properly handled, giving you time to relax and enjoy the wedding of your dreams. The Cayman Islands Department of Tourism also keeps a list of recommended independent wedding coordinators. Or you can order the brochure "Getting Married in the Cayman Islands" from Government Information Services. You can choose from many different styles of services or rewrite one as you wish.

Legal Requirements. Documentation can be prepared ahead of time or in one day while on the island. A minimal residency waiting period, blood test, and shots are not required.

You need to supply a Cayman Islands international embarkation/disembarkation card, as well as proof of identity (a passport or certified copy of your birth certificate signed by a notary public), and age (those under 18 must provide parental consent). If you've been married before, you must provide proof of divorce with the original or certified copy of the divorce decree if applicable, or a copy of the death certificate if your previous spouse died. You must list a marriage officer on the application, and you need at least two witnesses; if you haven't come with friends or family, the marriage officer can help you with that, too. A marriage license costs CI$200 (US$250).

Photographs. Deciding whether to use the photographer supplied by your resort or an independent photographer is an important choice. Resorts that host a lot of weddings usually have their own photographers, but you can also find independent, professional island-based photographers, and an independent wedding planner will know the best in the area.

THE HONEYMOON

If you choose to honeymoon at a resort, you can spend it getting champagne and strawberries delivered to your room each morning, floating in a swimming pool each afternoon, and dining in a five-star restaurant at night. Grand

Cayman offers resort options in different price ranges. Whether you want a luxurious experience or a more modest one, you'll certainly find someplace romantic to which you can escape. For a more secluded stay, opt for a private vacation-rental home or condo.

WEDDING RESOURCES

Deputy Chief Secretary. ⊠ *Government Admin Bldg., 3rd fl., George Town* ☎ *345/949–7900, 345/914–2222* ⊕ *www.gov. ky/about-us/our-government/ chief-officers.*

District Commissioner's Office. ⊠ *District Admin Bldg., 19 Kirkconnell St., Stake Bay* ☎ *345/948–2222, 345/948–2506* ⊕ *www.districtadmin. gov.ky.*

Government Information Services. ⊠ *Government Admin Bldg., Cricket Sq., 2nd fl., George Town* ☎ *345/949–8092* ⊕ *www.gis.gov.ky.*

Best Tours

A sightseeing tour is a good way to get your bearings and to experience Caymanian culture. Taxi drivers will give you a personalized tour of Grand Cayman for about $25 per hour for up to three people. Or you can choose a fascinating helicopter ride, a horseback- or mountain-bike journey, a 4x4 safari expedition, or a full-day bus excursion. The prices vary according to the mode of travel and the number and kind of attractions included. Ask your hotel to help you make arrangements.

GUIDED TOURS

Costs and itineraries for island tours are about the same regardless of the tour operator. Half-day tours average $40–$50 a person and generally include a visit to Hell and the Turtle Farm aquatic park in West Bay, as well as shopping downtown. Full-day tours ($60–$90 per person) add lunch, a visit to Bodden Town (the first settlement), and the East End, where you stop at the Queen Elizabeth II Botanic Park, blowholes (if the waves are high) on the ironshore, the Crystal Caves, and the site of the wreck of the *Ten Sails* (not the wreck itself—just the site). The pirate graves in Bodden Town were destroyed during Hurricane Ivan in 2008, and the blowholes were partially filled. Children under 12 often receive discounts.

Cayman Safari. This hits the usual sights but emphasizes interaction with locals, so you learn about craft traditions, folklore, and herbal medicines; careening along in Land Rovers is incidental fun. Rates range from $79 to $99 ($69 to $79 for children under 12). Take a trip to the Crystal caves also. ☎ 345/925–3002 ⊕ www. caymansafari.com.

Majestic Tours. The company caters mostly to cruise-ship and incentive groups but offers similar options to individuals and can customize tours, starting at $45 per person as well as pick you up at your lodging; it's particularly good for West Bay, including the Cayman Turtle Centre and Hell. ☎ 345/949–7773 ⊕ www. majestictours.ky.

McCurley Tours. This outfit is owned by B. A. McCurley, a free-spirited, freewheeling midwesterner who's lived in Cayman since the mid-1980s and knows everything and everyone on the East End. Not only is she encyclopedic and flexible, but she also offers car rentals and transfers for travelers staying on the North Side or East End; don't be surprised if she tells you what to order at lunch, especially if it's off the menu ☎ 345/947–9626, 345/916–0925 mobile phone ✉ mccurley@cwhiptop.com.

Tropicana Tours. Tropicana Tours offers several excellent Cayman highlights itineraries on its larger buses, including Stingray City stops, as well as reef-runner adventures across the North Sound through the mangrove swamps. ☎ 345/949–0944.

SPECIAL-INTEREST TOURS

Cayman Safari. Cayman Safari's 4WD tours hit the usual sights but emphasize interaction with locals, so you learn about craft traditions, folklore, and herbal medicines. ☎ 345/925–3002 ⊕ www.caymansafari.com.

Cayman Island Helicopters. Cayman Island Helicopters offers exhilarating eagle-eye views on three itineraries: $79 for a flyover of Seven Mile Beach; $145 for a trip adding Stingray City; and $355 for a thrillingly panoramic island-wide aerial tour (discounts are available if you book via the company's website, and shuttle service is free). Though the island is flat and mostly arid, the sight of waters rippling from turquoise to tourmaline is exciting enough. ☎ 345/943–4354, 345/926–6967 ⊕ www.caymanislandshelicopters.com.

On the Calendar

January

Cayman Cookout. Grand Cayman's most loved and most revered food festival, Cayman Cookout at the Ritz-Carlton Grand Cayman, draws in award-winning, celebrity chefs like Eric Ripert, Jose Andreas, and Emeril Lagasse. Dubbed "The Culinary Event of The Year," and rightly so, it gives you the opportunity to sip rum punches under the stars, brush up on your sommelier skills, and indulge in exquisite fine foods from some of the best chefs in the world. ⊕ *caymancookout. com*

February

Red Sky at Night. This is a favorite of participants and attendees alike. Witness live, immersive performances from musicians, dancers, actors, and storytellers, and meander through displays of creative work by visual artists and artisans in the F. J. Harquail Cultural Centre gardens. Revel in the sounds of steel pan, fiddle, and drums, and the aroma of mouthwatering local culinary delicacies. ⊕ *www.artscayman. org/red-sky-at-night*

Taste of Cayman. What started as a chili cook off in a field has now evolved to become Cayman's largest culinary celebration, Taste of Cayman attracts 45 restaurants to the green in Camana Bay for a foodie festival like no other. ⊕ *www. tasteofcayman.org*

May

Batabano & Cayman Carnival. The most colorful, vibrant festival in the Cayman Islands, Batabano is a street carnival where locals (and visitors) dance and "chip" down the road scantily clad in gigantic feathers and gem-embellished bikinis, all in the name of soca. Batabano is a time for people of all different descents to gather with a common interest and celebrate community spirit. ⊕ *www. caymancarnival.com*

June

Flowers Sea Swim. This annual event draws both Olympic-level and casual swimmers. Around 900 people take part in the 1-mile swim that runs parallel to the Seven Mile Beach. ⊕ *flowersseaswim.com*

July

Constitution Day. Celebrate Constitution Day with a stunning firework display at Camana Bay harbor.

October

Cayman Rejuvinate. A mind, body, and soul festival sees wellness buffs flock to the Ritz-Carlton Grand Cayman to partake in food seminars, intimate meditations, and yoga sessions that will leave you refreshed, revived, and, of course, rejuvenated. Experts in mindfulness, nutrition, skincare, fitness, and more share knowledge against the backdrop of picture-perfect Seven Mile Beach. If you're looking for an energy boost or prioritizing self-care, this is not one to miss. ⊕ *caymanrejuvenate.com*

Pirates Week. A swash-buckling display of Cayman history and heritage, Pirates Week is an annual week-long celebration of everything scallywag. A dress-up carnival in the streets, fireworks, and local street food fill George Town for the benefit and amusement of both locals and visitors. ⊕ *www.piratesweekfestival.com*

December

Parade of Lights. A stunning display of lights on the water as boats float along the Camana Bay harbor draped in colorful lights, the parade of lights occurs every December has become a highly anticipated event for all. ⊕ *www.camanabay.com*

Great Itineraries

It's a shame that so few visitors (other than divers) spend time on more than one island in a single trip. If you have more than a week, you can certainly spend some quality time on both Grand Cayman and one of its Sister Islands.

IF YOU HAVE 3 DAYS

Ensconce yourself at a resort along Grand Cayman's **Seven Mile Beach,** spending your first day luxuriating on the sand. On Day 2, get your feet wet at **Stingray City and Sandbar** in West Bay, where you can feed the alien-looking gliders by hand. Splurge for a great dinner on your second night at **Blue by Eric Ripert.** On your last day, head into **George Town** for some shopping. Have lunch with scintillating harbor views at **Lobster Pot** or **Casanova** before soaking up some last rays of sun.

IF YOU HAVE 7 DAYS

Because divers need to decompress before their return flight, the last day should be spent sightseeing on Grand Cayman. **The Cayman Turtle Farm** is an expensive but exceptional marine theme park, and well worth a visit. On the East End, hike the pristine **Mastic Trail,** then stroll through the gorgeous grounds at **Queen Elizabeth II Botanic Park.** Spend your final morning in George Town, perhaps snorkeling **Eden Rock.**

If you need a break from Seven Mile Beach, spend a full day beachcombing at the savagely beautiful **Barkers** in West Bay. If you have a car, explore the East End natural attractions, and grab lunch at the **Lighthouse.** Head east another day to visit historic **Pedro St. James Castle;** drive through the original capital, **Bodden Town,** then spend the afternoon (lunch, swimming, and water sports) at **Cayman Kai/Rum Point.**

IF YOU HAVE 10 DAYS

With 10 days, you can spend time on two or even all three islands. Begin on Cayman Brac; after diving the **north coast** walls, **MV Capt. Keith Tibbetts,** and the **Lost City of Atlantis** (or just lying on the beach), save a morning to hike through the **Parrot Reserve** out to the **East End Lighthouse** for sensational views. You can also climb the Lighthouse Steps which lead to **Peter's Cave.** On Little Cayman, chill out picnicking on **Owen Island,** and don't miss the **Booby Pond Nature Reserve.** Spend at least two nights on Grand Cayman.

GEORGE TOWN AND ENVIRONS

Updated by
Monica Walton

⦿ Sights	🍴 Restaurants	🛏 Hotels	🛍 Shopping	🍸 Nightlife
★★★★☆	★★★★☆	★★★☆☆	★★★★★	★★★★★

NEIGHBORHOOD SNAPSHOT

TOP EXPERIENCES

■ **Duty-free shopping:** Bargain hunters will love meandering through the plentiful shops.

■ **Eating out:** Marvel at the stunning harbor views while chowing down on local delicacies.

■ **Shore diving:** Two of Cayman's best shallow dives are in this district: Eden Rock and Devil's Grotto.

■ **Great cafés:** Cayman is home to nearly 20 trendy cafés, fueling a rampant caffeine culture that rivals Seattle.

■ **The National Museum:** Learn about Cayman at the National Museum that's almost 200 years old.

■ **Flightseeing:** View the stunning island from the air on a ride with Cayman Islands Helicopters.

GETTING HERE

George Town is a quick, five-minute car or taxi ride from Seven Mile Beach, or a 20-minute walk. The WB1 bus (with a yellow circle) will shuttle you between West Bay, Seven Mile Beach, and George Town, while the number 3 (purple) will take you between the airport, George Town, and West Bay. To get around the capital there's a free hop-on/hop-off shuttle that runs on a continuous loop around George Town on weekdays from 8 am to 6 pm from the depot by the courthouse. You'll find parking at Kirk Parking Lot on Albert Panton Street and behind Bayshore Mall.

QUICK BITES

■ **Brasserie Market.** The market is always packed. Get some coffee or tea, or design your own wrap or salad. ✉ *Cricket Sq., 171 Elgin Ave.* ☎ *345/945–1815* ⊕ *brasseriecayman. com.*

■ **Bread and Chocolate.** This easygoing vegan café whips up simply glorious plant-based plates. Or just get a flat white (with almond milk), home-grown kombucha, or vegan cookie. ✉ *3 Dr. Roy's Dr.* ☎ *345/945–3586* ⊕ *www.cafe.ky.*

■ **Cayman Cabana1.** This rustic, waterfront bar is popular for sunset drinks, nightly farm-to-fork dinners, and delicious local offerings like conch fritters, wild snapper, and lobster. ✉ *53 N. Church St., on waterfront* ☎ *345/949–3080* ⊕ *www.caymanca-banarestaurant. com.*

The country's mesmerizing and rich capital, George Town, is steeped in history and awash with pastel-color storefronts. It's the very heart of the Cayman Islands. This vibrant, duty-free shopping and business hub is home to charming coffee shops, must-do happy hours, and some of the finest waterfront dining on Grand Cayman. It's also where cruise ships disembark their passengers from tenders (the ships themselves typically moor outside the immediate harbor area).

Once the home of the first permanent settlement on Grand Cayman, George Town now dances to the beat of its own drum. Beyond the historic port, you'll find a wide variety of souvenir and jewelry stores as well as plenty of Caribbean curiosities around each sun-drenched bend. For starters, check out the The Cayman National Museum, which used to be the Old Court House, jail, and post office; it's now home to a collection of local artifacts, artwork, and intriguing historical information about the Cayman Islands.

Decorated with fishermen's huts, the ruins of an 18th-century fort and fish shacks dipped in dazzlingly bright lacquers of paint, George Town is the place to people-watch, shop for delightfully unique crafts from the craft market, set off on a cruise to explore the harbor, eat in casual (yet sophisticated) Caribbean restaurants, and enjoy a wealth of culture. While you're here, indulge in local delicacies, including the national dish, turtle stew. Photographers should bring their cameras for the harbor views.

Sights

Begin exploring the capital by strolling along the waterfront, Harbour Drive, to **Elmslie Memorial United Church,** named after the first Presbyterian missionary to serve in the Caymans. Its vaulted timber ceiling (built from salvaged wreck material in the shape of an upside-down hull), wooden arches, mahogany pews, and tranquil nave reflect the island's deeply religious nature.

George Town and Environs

Caribbean Sea

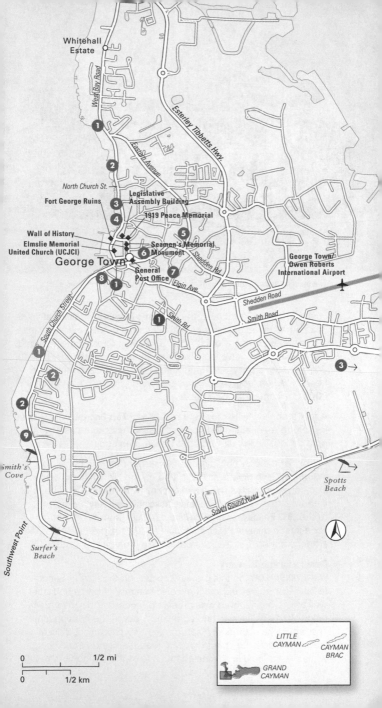

Whitehall Estate

West Bay Road

Esterley Tibbetts Hwy.

Eastern Avenue

North Church St.

Legislative
Assembly Building

Fort George Ruins

1919 Peace Memorial

Wall of History
Elmslie Memorial
United Church (UCJCI)

George Town

Seamen's Memorial
Monument

General
Post Office

George Town/
Owen Roberts
International Airport

Shedden Rd.

Elgin Ave.

Shedden Road

Smith Rd.

Smith Road

South Church Street

Smith's
Cove

Spotts Beach

Southwest Point

South Sound Road

Surfer's
Beach

LITTLE
CAYMAN

CAYMAN
BRAC

GRAND
CAYMAN

0   1/2 mi
0   1/2 km

The building housing the Cayman Islands National Museum has been a courthouse, a jail, and even a dance hall.

Just north near Fort Street, the **Seamen's Memorial Monument** lists 153 names on an old navigational beacon; a bronze piece by Canadian sculptor Simon Morris, titled *Tradition,* honors the almost 500 Caymanians who have lost their lives at sea. Dive-industry pioneer Bob Soto, wife Suzy, and daughter-in-law Leslie Bergstrom spearheaded the project, which Prince Edward unveiled during the 2003 quincentennial celebrations.

A few steps away lie the scant remains of **Fort George,** constructed in 1790 to repel plundering pirates; it also functioned as a watch post during World War II to scan for German subs.

In front of the court building, in the center of town, names of influential Caymanians are inscribed on the **Wall of History,** which also commemorates the islands' quincentennial. Across the street is the Cayman Islands **Legislative Assembly Building,** next door to the **1919 Peace Memorial Building.** A block south is the horseshoe-shape **General Post Office,** built in 1939 at the tail end of the art deco period. Let the kids pet the big blue iguana statues.

Cayman Islands Brewery
WINERY/DISTILLERY | In this brewery occupying the former Stingray facility, tour guides explain the iconic imagery of bottle and label as well as the nearly three-week brewing process: 7 days' fermentation, 10 days' lagering (storage), and 1 day in the bottling tank. The brewery's ecofriendly features are also championed: local farmers receive the spent grains to feed their cattle at no charge, while waste liquid is channeled into one of the Caribbean's most

advanced water-treatment systems. Then, enjoy your complimentary tasting knowing that you're helping the local environment and economy. The little shop also offers cute merchandise and a happening happy hour that lures locals for liming (as a sign prominently chides: "No working during drinking hours"). ⊠ *366 Shamrock Rd., Prospect, George Town* ☎ *345/947–6699* ⊕ *cib.ky* ⊠ *$10.*

★ Cayman Islands National Museum

HISTORIC SITE | FAMILY | Built in 1833, the historically significant clapboard home of the national museum has had several different incarnations over the years, serving as courthouse, jail, post office, and dance hall. It features an ongoing archaeological excavation of the Old Gaol and excellent 3-D bathymetric displays, murals, dioramas, and videos that illustrate local geology, flora and fauna, and island history. The first floor focuses on natural history, including a microcosm of Cayman ecosystems, from beaches to dry woodlands and swamps, and offers such interactive elements as a simulated sub. Upstairs, the cultural exhibit features renovated murals, video history reenactments, and 3-D back panels in display cases holding thousands of artifacts ranging from a 14-foot catboat with animatronic captain to old coins and rare documents. These paint a portrait of daily life and past industries, such as shipbuilding and turtling, and stress Caymanians' resilience when they had little contact with the outside world. There are also temporary exhibits focusing on aspects of Caymanian culture, a local art collection, and interactive displays for kids. ⊠ *3 Harbour Dr., George Town* ☎ *345/949–8368* ⊕ *www.museum.ky* ⊠ *$8* ۞ *Closed Sun.*

★ National Trust for the Cayman Islands

INFO CENTER | This office provides a map of historic and natural attractions, books and guides to Cayman, and information on its website about everything from iguanas to schoolhouses. The expanded gift shop provides one-stop souvenir shopping, from hair clips to logwood carvings to coconut soaps, all made on the island. Regularly scheduled activities range from boat tours through the forests of the Central Mangrove Wetlands, to cooking classes with local chefs, to morning walking tours of historic George Town. The office is walkable from George Town, but be aware that it's a 20-minute hike from downtown, often in the heat. ⊠ *Dart Park, 558 S. Church St., George Town* ☎ *345/749–1121* ⊕ *www.nationaltrust.org.ky.*

Beaches

Smith's Cove

BEACH—SIGHT | South of the Grand Old House, this tiny but popular protected swimming and snorkeling spot makes a wonderful

Maritime Heritage Trail

The National Trust for the Cayman Islands, National Museum, National Archive, Sister Islands Nature Tourism Project, and Department of the Environment have collaborated on a series of land-based sightseeing trails on Grand Cayman and the Sister Islands that commemorate the country's maritime heritage. Shoreside signs around the islands denote points of access and explain their historic or natural significance, from shipwreck sites to shorebird-sighting spots, chandlers' warehouses to lighthouses.

Brochures and posters are available at the National Trust and tourism offices on each island, as well as at many hotels. They provide additional information on turtling, shipbuilding, salvaging, fishing, and other sea-based economies. The project provides visitors with interactive and educational entertainment as they explore the islands.

beach wedding location. The bottom drops off quickly enough to allow you to swim and play close to shore. Although slightly rocky (its pitted limestone boulders resemble Moore sculptures), there's little debris and few coral heads, plenty of shade, picnic tables, restrooms, and parking. Surfers will find decent swells just to the south. Note the curious obelisk cenotaph "In memory of James Samuel Webster and his wife Arabella Antoinette (née Eden)," with assorted quotes from Confucius to John Donne. **Amenities:** parking (no fee); toilets. **Best for:** snorkeling; sunset; swimming. ⊠ Off S. Church St., George Town.

Spotts Beach

BEACH—SIGHT | On weekends families often barbecue at this idyllic spot caught between ironshore cliffs and a barrier reef (with fine snorkeling). You might even see some wild turtles swimming here. Follow South Church Street through South Sound past Red Bay; at a little cemetery there's a turnoff to the beach with a car park. **Amenities:** none. **Best for:** snorkeling; solitude; sunrise; walking. ⊠ Shamrock Rd., Spotts, George Town ✛ 1 mile east of East-West Arterial Rd. intersection.

Surfer's Beach

BEACH—SIGHT | Sitting pretty along the South Sound, Surfer's Beach lures surfers and skimboarders to its occasional herculean waves and soft shoreline. Perfectly positioned for swell when there's a cold front, it's usually deserted and quiet, adding to its undeniable allure. This pristine coastline is ideal for watching

Smith's Cove is a very popular, protected cove for swimming and snorkeling.

adrenaline junkies ride the waves, sunbathing in solitude, and, at the end of the day, watching the sun dipping into the turquoise-streaked sea. **Amenities:** parking (free). **Best for:** solitude, sunset, surfing. ⊠ *South Sound, George Town.*

🍴 Restaurants

You'll find a fair number of restaurants in George Town, including such standbys as Guy Harvey's and Casanova, not to mention the splurge-worthy Grand Old House.

★ The Brasserie

$$$ | **ECLECTIC** | Actuaries, bankers, and CEOs frequent this contemporary throwback to a colonial country club for lunch and "attitude adjustment" happy hours for creative cocktails and complimentary canapés. Inviting fusion farm/sea-to-table cuisine, emphasizing local ingredients whenever possible (the restaurant has its own boat and garden), includes terrific bar tapas. **Known for:** locavore's delight; creative small plates; power-broker hangout. ⑤ *Average main: $29* ⊠ *171 Elgin Ave., Cricket Sq., George Town* ☎ *345/945–1815* ⊕ *www.brasseriecayman.com* ⊘ *Closed weekends.*

Casanova Restaurant by the Sea

$$$ | **ITALIAN** | Owner Tony Crescente and younger brother, maitre d' Carlo, offer a simpatico dining experience, practically exhorting you to *mangia* and sending you off with a chorus of ciaos. There's some decorative *formaggio* (cheese): murals of grape clusters and

cavorting cherubs, paintings of the Amalfi Coast, and *una finestra sul mare* ("window to the sea") stenciled redundantly over arches opening onto the harbor. **Known for:** sensational harbor views; simpatico service; particularly fine sauces. $ *Average main: $30 ⊠ 65 N. Church St., George Town* ☎ *345/949–7633 ⊕ www.casanova.ky.*

Champion House II

$$ | CARIBBEAN | Ads trumpet that this restaurant overlooking a garden with a cheery tropical motif is "where the islanders dine"; indeed they have since the Robinson family started selling takeout from its kitchen in 1965. The West Indies breakfast, themed lunch, and Taste of Cayman dinner buffets are legendary spreads. **Known for:** traditional local and Asian dishes; lavish buffets; varied menu. $ *Average main: $20 ⊠ 43 Eastern Ave., George Town* ☎ *345/949–7882, 345/916–5736 ⊕ www.championhouse.ky* ⊘ *Closed Sat. No dinner Sun.*

Da Fish Shack

$$$ | SEAFOOD | This classic clapboard seaside shanty couldn't be homier: constructed from an old fishing vessel, the structure is an authentic representation of original Caymanian architecture. The deck is perfectly placed to savor the breezes and water views, and the chill Caribbean vibe makes it feel as if you're having the freshest seafood at a friend's home. **Known for:** terrific harbor views; delectable fish tacos; mellow ambience. $ *Average main: $25 ⊠ 127 N. Church St., George Town* ☎ *345/947–8126.*

★ Grand Old House

$$$$ | EUROPEAN | Built in 1908 as the Petra Plantation House and transformed into the island's first upscale establishment decades ago, this grande dame evokes bygone grandeur sans pretension. The interior rooms, awash in crystal, recall its plantation-house origins. **Known for:** elegant historic setting; comparatively affordable waterside tapas bar; classic continental fare with island twists. $ *Average main: $48 ⊠ 648 S. Church St., George Town* ☎ *345/949–9333 ⊕ www.grandoldhouse.com* ⊘ *Closed Sept. and Sun. in low season. No lunch weekends.*

Guy Harvey's Island Grill

$$$$ | SEAFOOD | This stylish upstairs bistro has mahogany furnishings, ship's lanterns, porthole windows, fishing rods, and Harvey's action-packed marine art. Seasonally changing dishes are peppered with Caribbean influences and the seafood is carefully chosen to exclude overexploited and threatened species. **Known for:** affordable nightly specials; terrific tapas; luscious lobster bisque. $ *Average main: $40 ⊠ Aquaworld Duty-Free Mall, 55 S. Church St., George Town* ☎ *345/946–9000.*

Farm Fresh

A joint initiative of the Cayman Islands Agricultural Society, the Ministry of Agriculture, the Department of Agriculture, and local vendors-purveyors, the **Market at the Grounds** is a jambalaya of sights, sounds, and smells held every Saturday from 7 am at the Stacy Watler Agricultural Pavilion in Lower Valley (East End). Local growers, fishers, home gardeners and chefs (dispensing scrumptious, cheap cuisine), and artisans display their wares in a tranquil green setting. To preserve Caymanian flavor, everything must be 100% locally grown. Participating craftspeople and artists, from couturiers to musicians, must use local designs and materials whenever possible. The market fosters a renewed spirit of community, providing literal feedback into the production process, while the interaction with visitors promotes understanding of island culture.

Lobster Pot

$$$$ | **SEAFOOD** | The nondescript building belies the lovely marine-motif decor and luscious seafood at this second-story restaurant overlooking the harbor. Enjoy lobster prepared several ways (all à la sticker shock) along with reasonably priced wine, which you can sample by the glass in the cozy bar. **Known for:** scintillating harbor views; strong selection of wines by the glass; predictably fine lobster, especially the Friday special lobster burger. ⑤ *Average main: $53* ⊠ *245 N. Church St., George Town* ☎ *345/949–2736* ⊕ *www.lobsterpot.ky* ☺ *No lunch weekends.*

MacDonald's

$ | **CARIBBEAN** | One of the locals' favorite burger joints—not a fast-food outlet—MacDonald's does a brisk lunch business in stick-to-your-ribs basics like rotisserie chicken and escoveitch fish. The decor features yellows and pinks, with appetizing posters of food and a large cartoon chicken mounted on the wall—all an afterthought, really, to the politicos, housewives in curlers, and gossipmongers. **Known for:** popular islander hangout; perennial local pick for best burger; juicy rotisserie chicken. ⑤ *Average main: $11* ⊠ *99 Shedden Rd., George Town* ☎ *345/949–4640.*

The Wharf

$$$$ | **SEAFOOD** | The popularity of this large restaurant often leads to impersonal service and mediocre food, though the Grand Old House management improved both after taking over in 2017; stick to such standards as conch fritters with spicy red pepper remoulade, and avoid anything sounding too pretentious. The

The Wharf is an enduring and popular restaurant on the waterfront on the outskirts of George Town.

location, a series of elevated decks and Victorian-style gazebos in blue and white hugging the sea, is enviable and helps to explain its enduring appeal; (wedding parties have their own pavilion, but celebrations of all sorts can overrun the place, including Salsa Tuesdays with lessons). **Known for:** stunning seaside location; fun evening entertainment including tarpon feedings; delectable desserts. *$ Average main: $44 ⊠ 43 W. Bay Rd., George Town ☎ 345/949–2231 ⊕ www.wharf.ky ⊗ No lunch weekends.*

☕ Coffee and Quick Bites

Coffee Point Cayman
$ | ECLECTIC | On the surprisingly large, eclectic Asian-tinged menu using ultrafresh ingredients, standouts include homemade carrot cake, mango smoothies, cranberry-Brie-pecan salad, and rosemary-roasted portobello and pesto chicken panini. The espresso martini will perk up anyone wanting a pick-me-up. **Known for:** creative beverages (alcoholic and non); delectable sandwiches; colorful local art. *$ Average main: ⊠ Pasadora Pl. at Smith Rd., George Town ☎ 345/946–1956, 345/814–0157 ⊕ coffeepoint.ky.*

🛏 Hotels

If you are looking for a cheaper option and are willing to forego a beachfront location, there are a couple of guesthouses and simple hotels around George Town.

Eldemire's Tropical Island Inn

$ | **B&B/INN** | You're about 15 minutes from Seven Mile Beach at this guesthouse south of George Town but less than 1 mile (1½ km) north of Smith Cove Beach. **Pros:** authentic Cayman hospitality and feel; inexpensive (with constant deals and discounts for paying cash); coin-operated laundry; free Wi-Fi. **Cons:** hard to find; slightly run-down; not on the beach; cleaning fee and minimum booking required (seven nights Christmas/New Year's, five nights high season, three rest of year). ⑤ *Rooms from: $157* ✉ *18 Pebbles Way, George Town* ⊹ *Off S. Church St.* ☎ *345/916–2022, 345/916–8369 reservations, 704/469–2635 toll-free in U.S.* ⊕ *www.eldemire.com* 🛏 *8 units* ⑩ *No meals* ☞ *3-night minimum stay.*

Sunset House

$$ | **HOTEL** | This amiable seaside dive-oriented resort is on the ironshore south of George Town, close enough for a short trip to stores and restaurants yet far enough to feel secluded. **Pros:** great shore diving and dive shop; lively bar scene; fun international clientele. **Cons:** five-night minimum stay required in high season; spotty Wi-Fi signal; no real swimming beach. ⑤ *Rooms from: $319* ✉ *390 S. Church St., George Town* ☎ *345/949–7111, 800/854–4767* ⊕ *www.sunsethouse.com* 🛏 *36 units* ⑩ *Free breakfast* ☞ *5-night minimum stay in winter.*

Nightlife

BARS AND MUSIC CLUBS

Cayman Cabana

BARS/PUBS | The popular restaurant and bar (formerly Hammerheads), adorned with wild murals, fab old-timer photos, and surfboards doubling as signs, offers a classic Cayman sight: fishers anchor their boats right offshore and display their catch right outside (condo and villa renters, head here if you're in the market for fresh fish). The capable kitchen specializes in classic Caymanian cuisine; farm-to-table Thursdays are justifiably popular. This is also a prime pyrotechnic sunset- and cruise ship watching spot, where locals laze in locally carved chairs, sipping house microbrews on the vast thatch-shaded, tiered deck. Stop by the Swanky Shack by the entrance for souvenir T-shirts and island gossip. ✉ *N. Church St., George Town* ☎ *345/949–3080, 345/938–1345* ⊕ *www.caymancabanarestaurant.com.*

Hard Rock Café

BARS/PUBS | Grand Cayman's Hard Rock replicates its 137-odd brethren around the world, especially on the weekends, only with more specialty drinks (try the Orangelicious margarita with

Monin pomegranate and blood-orange juices) to complement its extensive burger selection. A 1960 pink Cadillac, a Madonna bullet bra, and rotating memorabilia (gold records, costumes, guitars, and autographed photos from Elton John, Korn, John Lennon, U2, and *NSYNC) are the decor. ⊠ *43 S. Church St., George Town* ☎ *345/947–2020* ⊕ *www.hardrock.com.*

Margaritaville

BARS/PUBS | Grand Cayman's Margaritaville is a vast upstairs space that usually bustles with life (especially down its Green Monster waterslide or by its rooftop pool); the Friday evening happy hour is especially popular, with an overgrown frat-party atmosphere, and though drinks may be a bit pricier than at other waterfront locations, the jollity, 25 TVs, surprisingly tasty tacos, and free Wi-Fi definitely compensate. It closes early except on Friday night. ⊠ *Anchorage Center, 32 Harbour Dr., 2nd fl., George Town* ☎ *345/949–6274* ⊕ *www.margaritavillecaribbean.com* ☽ *Closed Sun.*

My Bar

BARS/PUBS | Perched on the water's edge, this bar has great sunset views. The leviathan open-sided cabana is drenched in Rasta colors and crowned by an intricate South Seas–style thatched roof with about 36,000 palm fronds. Christmas lights and the occasional customer dangle from the rafters. They offer great grub, and the crowd is a mischievous mix of locals, expats, and tourists. ⊠ *Sunset House, S. Church St., George Town* ☎ *345/949–7111* ⊕ *www.sunsethouse.com.*

The Office Lounge

BARS/PUBS | This is indeed a preferred hangout for the diverse after-work crowd, which packs both the cozy club space (adorned with customers' ties) and breezy patio, absorbing the high-octane cocktails and nightly musical mix (from country to salsa, karaoke to live bands). Happy hours are joyous indeed with CI$5 martini specials. It's invariably lively—a favorite spot for birthday, office, and bachelor and bachelorette parties and a prime place to eavesdrop on local gossip. ⊠ *99 Shedden Rd., George Town* ☎ *345/945–5212* ⊕ *www.tropicports.com/theoffice.*

Rackam's Waterfront Pub and Restaurant

BARS/PUBS | Both fishermen and financiers savor sensational sunsets and joyous happy hours, then watch tarpon feeding at this open-air, marine-theme bar on a jetty. Boaters and snorkelers, before and after checking out the wreck of *The Cali,* cruise up the ladder for drinks, while anglers leave their catch on ice. There's complimentary snacks on Friday and pub fare at fair prices until midnight. ⊠ *93 N. Church St., George Town* ☎ *345/945–3860* ⊕ *www.rackams.com.*

The Wharf

BARS/PUBS | Dance near the water to mellow music on Saturday evening; when there's a wedding reception in the pavilion, the crashing surf and twinkling candles bathe the proceedings in an almost Gatsby-esque glow. For something less sedate, try salsa lessons and dancing on Tuesday after dinner; most Fridays morph into a wild 1970s disco night (after the free hors d'oeuvres served during happy hour). The legendary Barefoot Man (think a Jimmy Buffett–style expat) performs Saturday. The stunning seaside setting on tiered decks compensates for often undistinguished food and service. The Ports of Call bar is a splendid place for sunset, and tarpon feeding off the deck happens nightly at 7 and 9. ⊠ *43 West Bay Rd., George Town* ☎ *345/949–2231* ⊕ *www.wharf.ky.*

🎭 Performing Arts

VENUES
Lions Centre

ARTS CENTERS | The center hosts events throughout the year: Battle of the Bands competitions, concerts by top names on the Caribbean and international music scene such as Maxi Priest, stage productions, pageants, and sporting events. ⊠ *905 Crewe Rd., Red Bay Estate, George Town* ☎ *345/945–4667, 345/949–7211.*

Prospect Playhouse

THEATER | A thrust proscenium stage allows the Cayman Drama Society and its partner arts organizations to mount comedies, musicals, and dramas (original and revival) year-round. ⊠ *223B Shamrock Rd., Prospect, George Town* ☎ *345/947–1998, 345/949–5054* ⊕ *www.cds.ky.*

🛍️ Shopping

ART GALLERIES

The art scene has exploded in the past decade, moving away from typical Caribbean motifs and "primitive" styles. Cayman's most famous artist had been the late Gladwyn Bush, fondly known as Miss Lassie, who died in 2003. She began painting her intuitive religious subjects after a vision she had when she was 62. She also decorated the facade, interior walls, furnishings, even appliances of her home, which was converted into a museum and workshop space, The Mind's Eye, at the junction of South Shore Road and Walkers Road. Bush was awarded the MBE (Most Excellent Order of the British Empire) in 1997, and her work is

Caymans Captivating Carnival

Held annually during the first week of May (or the week after Easter), the four-day **Batabano Cayman Carnival** (⊕ *www.caymancarnival.com*) is the island's boisterous answer to Mardi Gras, not to mention Carnival in Rio and Trinidad. Though not as hedonistic, the pageantry, electricity, and enthralled throngs are unrivaled (except for during Pirates Week). Events include a carnival ball, soca and calypso song competitions, massive Mas (masquerade) parade with ornate floats, street dance, and a beach fete. The festivities are enhanced by tasty concession stands offering Caymanian and other Caribbean cuisine.

The word *batabano* refers to the tracks that turtles leave as they heave onto beaches to nest. Locating those tracks was reason to celebrate in the past, when turtling was a major part of the economy, so it seemed an appropriate tribute to the islands' heritage, alongside the traditional Caribbean celebration of the region's African roots. Indeed, many of the increasingly elaborate costumes are inspired by Cayman's majestic marine life and maritime history from parrots to pirates, though some offer provocative social commentary. Thousands of revelers line the streets each year cheering their favorite masqueraders and boogieing to the Mas steel pan and soca bands. The organizers also hold a stand-alone street parade for Cayman's youth called Junior Carnival Batabano the weekend before the adult parade. Equally exciting, it stresses the importance of teaching the art of costume making and Mas, ensuring Carnival will be a lasting custom.

found in collections from Paris to Baltimore, the latter of whose American Visionary Art Museum owns several canvases. Bendel Hydes is another widely respected local, who moved to SoHo more than two decades ago yet still paints Caymanian-inspired works that capture the islands' elemental colors and dynamic movement. Leading expat artists include Joanne Sibley and Charles Long, both of whom create more figurative Cayman-focused art, from luminous landscapes and shining portraits to pyrotechnically hued flora. Several artists' home-studios double as galleries, including the internationally known Al Ebanks, the controversial Luelan Bodden, and fanciful sculptor Horacio Esteban; the National Gallery has a full list.

Artifacts

ART GALLERIES | On the George Town waterfront, Artifacts sells Spanish pieces of eight, doubloons, and Halcyon Days enamels (hand-painted collectible pillboxes made in England), as well as antique maps and other collectibles. ⊠ *Cayside Courtyard, Harbour Dr., George Town* ☎ *345/949–2442* ⊕ *www.artifacts.com.ky.*

Cathy Church's Underwater Photo Centre and Gallery

ART GALLERIES | The store has a collection of the acclaimed underwater shutterbug's spectacular color and limited-edition black-and-white underwater photos as well as the latest marine camera equipment. Cathy will autograph her latest coffee-table book, talk about her globe-trotting adventures, and schedule private underwater photography instruction on her dive boat, with graphics-oriented computers to critique your work. She also does wedding photography, above and underwater. ⊠ *390 S. Church St., George Town* ☎ *345/949–7415* ⊕ *www.cathychurch.com.*

★ Guy Harvey's Gallery and Shoppe

ART GALLERIES | World-renowned marine biologist, conservationist, and artist Guy Harvey showcases his aquatic-inspired, action-packed art in every conceivable medium, from tableware to sportswear (even logo soccer balls and Zippos). The soaring, two-story 4,000-square-foot space is almost more theme park than store, with monitors playing sport-fishing videos, wood floors inlaid with tile duplicating rippling water, dangling catboats "attacked" by shark models, and life-size murals honoring such classics as Hemingway's *The Old Man and the Sea.* Original paintings, sculpture, and drawings are expensive, but there's something (tile art, prints, lithographs, and photos) in most price ranges. ⊠ *49 S. Church St., George Town* ☎ *345/943–4891* ⊕ *www.guyharvey.com* ⊙ *Closed Sun.*

Pure Art

ART GALLERIES | About 1½ miles (2½ km) south of George Town, Pure Art purveys wit, warmth, and whimsy from the wildly colored front steps. Its warren of rooms resembles a garage sale run amok or a quirky grandmother's attic spilling over with unexpected finds, from foodstuffs to functional and wearable art. ⊠ *S. Church St. and Denham-Thompson Way, George Town* ☎ *345/949–9133* ⊕ *www.pureart.ky.*

CIGARS

Given Cayman's proximity to Cuba, the banned but tempting panatelas and robustos are readily available at reasonable prices. They are still considered contraband in the United States until the embargo is lifted.

Churchill's Cigars

TOBACCO | A cigar-store Indian points the way into this tobacco emporium, which sells the island's largest selection of authentic

Native Sons: Caymanian Artists

In 1995 three artists founded a collaborative called Native Sons, adding a fourth in 1996, and currently featuring 10 members. Their primary goal is to develop and promote Caymanian artists. Though they work in different mediums and styles, the group resists facile characterization and challenges conventions as to what characterizes "Caribbean" art. One of the core members, Al Ebanks, has achieved major international success, but he admits that the islands can be provincial: "Cayman doesn't always recognize talent unless you're signed to a gallery overseas."

Though the National Gallery and the Cayman National Cultural Foundation both vigorously support the movement and are committed to sponsoring local artists, some Native Sons members feel their agendas can be too safe, ironically exemplifying the bureaucratic, corporate mentality they admit is often necessary to raise funds for nonprofit institutions. They have also felt subtle pressure to conform commercially and an inherent bias toward expat artists, whose work often depicts the literally sunnier side of Caymanian life, and resent what they perceived to be censorship of rawer, edgier works, including depictions of nudity in archconservative Cayman. They have sought to push the boundaries for both institutions and private galleries. "Yes, art is art and shouldn't be grounded in national stereotypes, though my country inspires my work. ... We just want balance," Ebanks says. "People look at more challenging work and ask 'Where are the boats?' We live that scene!"

Obviously this is a hot-button topic on a tiny island. Chris Christian, who originally achieved success through representational beach scenes but wanted to expand and experiment, uses the Cayman term "crabs in a bucket," describing how "artists in a small pool scratch and scramble over each other, succeeding by badmouthing others." Which is why the support structure and philosophy of Native Sons is so vital: They help each other negotiate "that constant balance between commercial success and artistic integrity."

Other members include cofounder Wray Banker, Randy Chollette, Nasaria Suckoo-Chollette, Gordon Solomon, Horacio Esteban, and Nickola McCoy. These native sons and daughters all passionately believe art isn't merely about pretty pictures, and uncompromisingly believe in preserving Caymanian culture and freedom of expression.

Cubanos (and other imports), including such names as Upmann, Romeo y Julieta, and Cohiba, displayed in the dark, clubby surroundings. The enthusiastic staff will advise on drink pairings (bold older rum for a Montecristo No. 2, cognac for smaller Partagas Shorts, a single-malt scotch such as Glenmorangie for the Bolivar Belicoso Fino). There's a small airport branch and one at the Kimpton Seafire Resort + Spa as well. ☒ *Island Plaza, Harbour Dr., George Town* ☎ *345/945–6141* ⊕ *www.churchillscigarscayman. com.*

CLOTHING
Blue Wave
CLOTHING | Blue Wave and Waterman surf and clothing shops have same owners (Waterman is in Seven Mile Beach). At the George Town shop you'll find brands like Billabong, Quicksilver, and Olukai, plus essentials like sandals, sunglasses, and surfboards. ☒ *10 Shedden Rd., George Town* ☎ *345/949–8166* ⊕ *www. watermancayman.ky.*

FOOD
There are seven modern, U.S.-style supermarkets (three of them have full-service pharmacies) on Grand Cayman owned by two different companies. Ask your hotel about which one is nearest you. Together, they will spoil you for choices of fresh fruit and vegetables, a wide selection of groceries, and a good selection of meats, poultry, and fish. All have deli counters serving hot meals, salads, sandwiches, cold cuts, and cheeses. Kirk Supermarket carries a wide range of international foods from the Caribbean, Europe, and Asia. The biggest difference you'll find between these and supermarkets on the mainland is the prices, which are about 25%–30% more than at home.

Kirk Supermarket and Pharmacy
FOOD/CANDY | This store is open Monday–Thursday 7 am–10 pm (11 pm Friday and Saturday) and is a particularly good source for traditional Caymanian fast food (oxtail, curried goat) and beverages at the juice bar. It also carries the largest selection of organic and special dietary products; the pharmacy (Monday–Saturday 8 am–9 pm) stocks homeopathic and herbal remedies. ☒ *413 Eastern Ave., near intersection with West Bay Rd., George Town* ☎ *345/949–7022* ⊕ *www.kirkmarket.ky* ☉ *Closed Sun.*

Tortuga Rum Company
FOOD/CANDY | This company bakes, then vacuum-seals more than 10,000 of its world-famous rum cakes daily, adhering to the original, "secret" century-old recipe. There are eight flavors, from banana to Blue Mountain coffee, as well as several varieties of candy, from taffy to truffles. The 12-year-old rum, blended from

Cayman Craft Market

This open-air marketplace run by the Tourism Attraction Board at Hog Sty Bay, smack in the middle of George Town, is artist central, helping maintain old-time Caymanian skills. The vendors offer locally made leather, thatch, wood, and shell items. You'll also find dolls, hats, carved parrots, bead and seed jewelry, hand-painted thatch bags and bonnets, and hand-carved waurie (also spelled warri) boards—an ancient African game using seeds or (more modernly) marbles.

Also available here are Sea Salt (and their luxury bath product); Hawley Haven Farm products (Mrs. Laurie Hawley's delectable papaya, tamarind, and guava jams; spicy mango chutney; thyme vinegar; Cayman honey; and jerk sauce; as well as her painted folkloric characters on handmade sundried paper made with native flowers, leaves, and herbs); the Cayman Tropicals line of fragrant fruit-based hair and skin-care products; and North Side's Whistling Duck Farm specialties, from soursop to sea grape jams and jellies. Every month highlights a different area of the Cayman Islands, from Cayman Brac to Bodden Town.

private stock though actually distilled in Guyana, is a connoisseur's delight for after-dinner sipping. You can buy a fresh rum cake at the airport on the way home at the same prices as at the factory store. ⊠ *Industrial Park, N. Sound Rd., George Town* ☎ *345/943–7663* ⊕ *www.tortugarumcakes.com.*

JEWELRY

Although you can find black-coral products in Grand Cayman, they're controversial. Most of the coral sold here comes from Belize and Honduras; Cayman Islands marine law prohibits the removal of live coral from its own sea. Black coral grows at a glacial rate (3 inches per decade) and is an endangered species. Cayman, however, is famed for artisans working with the material; shops are recommended, but let your conscience dictate your purchases.

★ Balaclava Jewellers

JEWELRY/ACCESSORIES | This shop is the domain of Martina and Philip Cadien, who studied at Germany's prestigious Pforzheim Goldsmithing School. The showroom sparkles appropriately, with breathtaking handcrafted pieces—usually naturally colored diamonds set in platinum or 18K white, yellow, and rose gold—framed and lovingly, almost sensuously lit. Although there are simpler strands, this is a place where flash holds sway; the prices take your breath away, but the gaudy gems are flawless. ⊠ *Governors Square, 23 Lime Tree Bay Ave., Seven Mile Beach* ☎ *345/945–5788* ⊕ *www.balaclava-jewellers.com* ☉ *Closed Sun.*

Island Jewellers

JEWELRY/ACCESSORIES | Locals appreciate Island Jewellers for its affordable line of watches, especially top-notch Swiss brands, from Movado to Marvin to Maurice Lacroix, and selection of stunning diamonds and jewelry There's another branch with similar inventory in the Flagship Building. ⊠ *Island Plaza, Cardinal Ave., George Town* ☎ *345/946–2333* ⊕ *www.islandjewellers.com.*

Magnum Jewelers

JEWELRY/ACCESSORIES | Befitting its name, Magnum Jewelers traffics in high-caliber pieces by the elite likes of Girard-Perregeaux and Harry Winston for a high-powered clientele. A talented team source distinctive contemporary watches and bijoux (especially increasingly rare colored diamonds) for their equally glittery celebrity clientele, who appreciate a bargain like the rest of us. Smaller spenders might appreciate whimsical items such as pendants with hand-painted enamel sandals or crystal-encrusted purses. ⊠ *Cardinal Plaza, Cardinal Ave., George Town* ☎ *345/946–9199* ⊕ *www.magnumjewelers.com.*

Rocky's Diamonds

JEWELRY/ACCESSORIES | In the heart of George Town owner Rakesh Baksani hand-picks only the most stunning and desirable rocks—emeralds, sapphires, tanzanite, and, of course, glittering diamonds. You'll find them all on display at competitive duty-free prices on the bustling waterfront in the country's capital. ⊠ *28 N. Church St., George Town* ☎ *345/546–6250, 345/946–7851* ⊕ *www.rockysdiamonds.com.*

LIQUOR

Cayman Spirits/Seven Fathoms Rum

WINE/SPIRITS | Surprisingly, this growing company, established in 2008, is Cayman's first distillery. It's already garnered medals in prestigious international competitions for its artisanal small-batch rums (and is now making a splash with its smooth Gun Bay vodka as well). You can stop by for a tasting and self-guided tour (a more intensive, extensive guided tour costs $15) to learn how the rum is aged at 7 fathoms (42 feet) deep; supposedly the natural motion of the currents maximizes the rum's contact with the oak, extracting its rich flavors and enhancing complexity. ⊠ *68 Bronze Rd., George Town* ☎ *345/925–5379, 345/926–8186* ⊕ *www. caymanspirits.com.*

SHOPPING CENTERS
Bayshore Mall
SHOPPING CENTERS/MALLS | Optimally located downtown and one of the leading shopaholics' targets (you can't miss the cotton-candy colors), this mall contains a Kirk Freeport department-store branch (Tag Heuer to Herend porcelain, Mikimoto to Mont Blanc), swank Lalique and Lladró boutiques, La Parfumerie (which often offers makeovers and carries 450 beauty brands), and other usual luxury culprits. ⊠ S. Church St., George Town.

Cayside Courtyard
SHOPPING CENTERS/MALLS | This small courtyard shopping center is noted for its specialty jewelers and antiques dealers. ⊠ Harbour Dr., George Town.

Duty Free Plaza
SHOPPING CENTERS/MALLS | This mall caters to more casual shoppers with the T-shirt Factory, Island Treasures, Havana Cigars, Blackbeard's Rumcake Bakery, and the Surf Shop. It also contains a kid-pleasing 12,000-gallon saltwater aquarium with sharks, eels, and stingrays. ⊠ S. Church St., George Town.

Island Plaza
SHOPPING CENTERS/MALLS | Here you'll find 15 duty- and tax-free stores, including Swarovski Boutique, Island Jewellers, and Churchill's Cigars (with bars like Margaritaville to de-stress in after binge shopping). ⊠ Harbour Dr., George Town.

Kirk Freeport Plaza
SHOPPING CENTERS/MALLS | This downtown shopping center, home to the Kirk Freeport flagship department store, is ground zero for couture; it's also known for its boutiques selling fine watches and jewelry, china, crystal, leather, perfumes, and cosmetics, from Baccarat to Bulgari, Raymond Weil to Waterford and Wedgwood (the last two share their own autonomous boutique). Just keep walking—there's plenty of eye-catching, mind-boggling consumerism in all directions: Boucheron, Cartier (with its own miniboutique), Chanel, Clinique, Christian Dior, Clarins, Estée Lauder, Fendi, Guerlain, Lancôme, Yves Saint Laurent, Issey Miyake, Jean Paul Gaultier, Nina Ricci, Rolex, Rosenthal and Royal Doulton china, and more. ⊠ Cardinal Ave., George Town.

Landmark
SHOPPING CENTERS/MALLS | Stores in the Landmark sell perfumes, treasure coins, and upscale beachwear; Breezes Bistro restaurant is upstairs. ⊠ Harbour Dr., George Town.

🐠 Activities

DIVING

George Town has two popular shore dive spots. **Devil's Grotto** resembles an abstract painting of anemones, tangs, parrotfish, and bright purple Pederson cleaner shrimp (nicknamed the dentists of the reef, as they gorge on whatever they scrape off fish teeth and gills). Extensive coral heads and fingers teem with blue wrasse, horse-eyed jacks, butterfly fish, and Indigo hamlets. The cathedral-like caves are phenomenal, but tunnel entries aren't clearly marked, so you're best off with a dive master.

If someone tells you that the silverside minnows are in at **Eden Rock,** drop everything and dive here. The schools swarm around you as you glide through the grottoes, forming quivering curtains of liquid silver as shafts of sunlight pierce the sandy bottom. The grottoes themselves are safe—not complex caves—and the entries and exits are clearly visible at all times. Snorkelers can enjoy the outside of the grottoes as the reef rises and falls from 10 to 30 feet deep. Avoid carrying fish food or risk getting bitten by eager yellowtail snappers.

DIVE OPERATORS

Cayman Aggressor IV

SCUBA DIVING | This 110-foot live-aboard dive boat offers one-week cruises for divers who want to get serious bottom time, as many as five dives daily. Nine staterooms with bathrooms en suite sleep 18. The fresh food is basic but bountiful (three meals, two in-between snacks), and the crew offers a great mix of diving, especially when weather allows the crossing to Little Cayman. Digital photography and video courses are also offered (there's an E-6 film-processing lab aboard) as well as nitrox certification. The price is $2,895 to $3,295 double occupancy for the week. ☎ 345/949-5551, 800/348-2628 ⊕ www.aggressor.com.

Deep Blue Divers

SCUBA DIVING | FAMILY | Two custom-designed 27-foot outward-driven Dusky boats ensure a smooth, speedy ride and can access sites that much larger boats can't. They accept a maximum of eight guests, under the watchful eyes of Nick Buckley, who jokes that diving is "relaxing under pressure." Personalized valet attention and flexibility bring a high repeat clientele; Nick's particularly good with kids and has taught three generations of families. He's often asked by happy customers to join them on dive trips around the world. He and his crew delight in telling stories about Cayman culture and history, including pirate tales and often hilarious anecdotes about life in the Cayman Islands. He offers underwater

Divers exploring one of Grand Cayman's famous reefs

photo–video services and a range of PADI-certified courses; beach pickup is included. ⊠ *245 N. Church St., George Town* ☎ *345/916–1293* ⊕ *www.deepbluediverscayman.com.*

Eden Rock Diving Center

SCUBA DIVING | South of George Town, this outfit provides easy access to Eden Rock and Devil's Grotto. It features full equipment rental, lockers, shower facilities, and a full range of PADI courses from a helpful, cheerful staff on its Pro 42 jet boat. ⊠ *124 S. Church St., George Town* ☎ *345/949–7243* ⊕ *www.edenrockdive.com.*

Sunset Divers

SCUBA DIVING | At a hostelry that caters to the scuba set, this full-service PADI teaching facility has great shore diving and seven dive boats (two added in 2019) that hit all sides of the island. Divers can be independent on boats as long as they abide by maximum time and depth standards. Instruction (in five languages, thanks to the international staff) and stay-dive packages are comparatively inexpensive. Though the company is not directly affiliated with acclaimed underwater shutterbug Cathy Church (whose shop is also at the hotel), she often works with the instructors on special courses. ⊠ *Sunset House, 390 S. Church St., George Town* ☎ *345/949–7111, 800/854–4767* ⊕ *www.sunsethouse.com.*

FISHING

Oh Boy Charters

FISHING | Charters include a 60-foot yacht with complete amenities (for day and overnight trips, sunset and dinner cruises) and a

Learning In-Depth

Technical diving refers to advanced dives conducted beyond the 130-foot depth limit, requiring a decompression stop, or into an overhead environment. DiveTech's Nancy Easterbrook compares it to "skiing a really steep mogul-ly double black diamond, or scaling a sheer cliff face. It takes practice and determination." The courses and equipment are also much more expensive.

Terms you'll soon hear are *Nitrox, Advanced Nitrox, Normoxic, Trimix,* and *Advanced Trimix.* These all enable divers to explore deeper depths safely at greater length. Nitrox, for example, is highly oxygenated nitrogen (32% as opposed to "normal" air, with 21%), which enables you to dive for a longer time before reaching decompression limits. And just like the oxygen-bar craze of the last decade, Nitrox invigorates you, reducing fatigue after dives.

Rebreather diving (Closed Circuit Rebreathers, or CCR) is another popular way to extend dive time, up to three hours 100 feet down. You breathe warmer, moister air (reducing the chance of chills at lower depths). As a bonus, denizens of the deep are less wary, as there are no bubbles.

34-foot Crusader. Charles and Alvin Ebanks—sons of Caymanian marine royalty, the indomitable Captain Marvin Ebanks—jokingly claim they've been playing in and plying the waters for a century and tell tales (tall and otherwise) of their father reeling them in for fishing expeditions. No more than eight passengers on the deep-sea boats ensures the personal touch (snorkeling on the 60-footer accommodates more people). Guests always receive a good selection of their catch; if you prefer others to do the cooking, go night fishing (including catch-and-release shark safaris), which includes dinner. ☎ 345/949–6341, 345/926–0898 ⊕ www. ohboycharters.com.

R&M Fly Shop and Charters
FISHING | FAMILY | Captain Ronald Ebanks is arguably the island's most knowledgeable fly-fishing guide, with more than 10 years' experience in Cayman and Scotland. He also runs light-tackle trips on a 25-foot Robalo and 21-foot Sea Cat. Everyone from beginners—even children—to experienced casters enjoy and learn, whether wading or poling from a 17-foot Stratos Flats boat or his new sleek 17-foot Hobie Pro Angler kayaks. Free transfers are included. Captain Ronald even ties his own flies (he'll show you how). ☎ 345/947–3146, 345/916–5753 mobile ⊕ www.flyfish-grandcayman.com.

HORSEBACK RIDING
Mary's Stables and Equestrian Center
HORSEBACK RIDING | The top-notch training facility for the Cayman national equestrian team offers classic English riding lessons (dressage and jumping are options) in three arenas and allows you to help groom the exotic horses. ☒ *Half Way Pond, George Town* ☎ *345/949–7360, 345/516–1751* ⊕ *www.equestriancenter.ky.*

SEA EXCURSIONS
Nautilus
BOATING | On this semisubmersible you can sit above deck or venture below, where you can view the reefs and marine life through a sturdy glass hull. A one-hour undersea tour is $60. Watch divers feed the fish, or take the Captain's Nemo's Tour that includes snorkeling; a catamaran cruise to Stingray City and land-sea tours are also offered. ☒ *93 N. Church St., George Town* ⊹ *Inside Rackam's* ☎ *345/945–1355.*

Sea Trek
BOATING | **FAMILY** | Helmet diving lets you walk and breathe 26 feet underwater for an hour—without getting your hair wet. No training or even swimming ability is required (ages eight and up), and you can wear glasses. Guides give a thorough safety briefing, and a sophisticated system of compressors and cylinders provides triple the amount of air necessary for normal breathing while a safety diver program ensures four levels of backup. The result at near-zero gravity resembles an exhilarating moonwalk ($89). ☒ *Cayman Cabana, 53 N. Church St., George Town* ☎ *345/949–0008* ⊕ *www. seatrekcayman.com, www.snubacayman.com.*

SKATING AND SKATEBOARDING
Black Pearl Skate and Surf Park
IN-LINE SKATING/ROLLER SKATING | **FAMILY** | Black Pearl Skate and Surf Park, (skateboards, in-line skates), is the size of a football field (at 52,000 square feet the world's second-largest such facility), with stairs and rails, plus a half pipe, 20-foot vert ramp, and flow course offering innumerable lies. International professional skaters such as Tony Hawk, Ryan Sheckler, and Mark Appleyard have practiced their kickflips, tailslides, wheelies, and grinds here. You can arrange lessons or rent anything you need at the adjacent skate–surf shop. Local daredevils often mount rad performances Friday and Saturday night. The park doesn't open until 3 pm. ☒ *Grand Harbour, Red Bay Rd., Red Bay Estate, George Town* ☎ *345/939–1301* ⊕ *www.blackpearl.ky.*

SEVEN MILE BEACH

Updated by
Monica Walton

⊙ **Sights**   🍴 **Restaurants**   🛏 **Hotels**   ⬤ **Shopping**   🍸 **Nightlife**
★★★★★   ★★★★★   ★★★★★   ★★★★★   ★★★★★

NEIGHBORHOOD SNAPSHOT

TOP EXPERIENCES

- **Beaches:** Waste away the day on the bleach-blonde sands of Seven Mile Beach, or sink into the soft sands of Governors beach.

- **Spas:** Grand Cayman is home to myriad bliss-inducing, world-class spas that will lull you into a state of pure relaxation.

- **Nightlife:** If a day in the sun hasn't taken it out of you, kick off your flip-flops and hit one of the island's beachfront bars any night of the week.

- **Sunset cruises:** Watch the sky light up like a fiery peach as you glide along the still waters of Grand Cayman.

- **Stingray city tour:** A must-do when you're in the Cayman Islands is a morning or afternoon boat trip to Stingray Sandbar.

GETTING HERE

Seven Mile Beach is a 15-minute taxi ride from the airport. The Camana Bay development sits almost in the middle. Most hotels offer shuttles to and from attractions, and buses (yellow and purple circles) run every few minutes for a fee of C$2 to C$5, making it easy to get around. It will take you around 20 minutes to walk along the strip.

PLANNING YOUR TIME

Everyone visiting Grand Cayman is bound to visit Seven Mile Beach, and it's safe at any time of day or night. Snag a souvenir from any of the plazas on West Bay Road. You'll never lack scrumptious eats. Parking is free in most plazas along the strip. Need a break from the hot sun? Take a dip in the cool, shallow waters.

QUICK BITES

- **Chicken Chicken.** Addictive, flavor-packed Caribbean wood-roasted chicken is what makes this spot a local favorite. ⊠ *West Shore Centre* ☎ 345/945–2290 ⊕ *www. chicken2.com.*

- **Coccoloba.** The perfect place to grab a quick bite without leaving the beach offers tacos, burgers, and salads with an uninterrupted view of Seven Mile Beach. ⊠ *Kimpton Seafire, 60 Tanager Way* ☎ 345/746–4111 ⊕ *www.seafireresortandspa.com.*

- **Paradise Pizza.** Neapolitan-style pizzas, shawarma, and flatbreads are served in a garden flanked with leafy palms and an authentic Italian brick oven. ⊠ *Palm Heights Hotel, 747 W. Bay Rd.* ☎ 345/949–3491 ⊕ *www.paradise. pizza.*

One of the Caribbean's most famed and luxurious beaches laughs in the face of generic sandy counterparts, trumping them all with its glittering whiter-than-white strip of beach. Easily the best beach in the Cayman Islands, it's sandwiched between dazzling cyan waters and dense green foliage, a gateway to the Caribbean sea beyond. Beaches don't come any more perfect than this.

But Seven Mile Beach is more than a beach. Although it's not exactly a "city," it's where the lion's share of Grand Cayman's tourist activity takes place. Year-round, Seven Mile Beach buzzes with culinary and cultural events like Batabano, Cayman Cookout, and Pirates Week. Swanky resorts, such as the Ritz-Carlton and Kimpton Seafire, line the shoreline, offering front-row seats to the famed 7-mile sunset. As night falls, the district is governed by pleasure, with bars and restaurants buzzing into the early hours of the morning.

After a quick 15-minute cab ride from the airport, you'll get your first glimpse of the famous shoreline. Many island visitors will be staying in this region, so they will have these views daily, but if your lodgings are elsewhere on Grand Cayman, this is definitely a place you'll want to visit. What will stun you first is the sheer amount of fish swimming around in its crystal clear waters. Bring your gear and dive in, or get your tan on in your own cabana. When your belly starts to rumble, you don't have to walk far to reach one of the few restaurants scattered along the coast, where you'll find caught-this-morning seafood and fresh juices or—if you prefer—cocktails to-die-for.

Sights

Camana Bay Observation Tower
VIEWPOINT | **FAMILY** | This 75-foot structure provides striking 360-degree panoramas of otherwise flat Grand Cayman, sweeping from George Town and Seven Mile Beach to the North Sound. The double-helix staircase is impressive in its own right. Running alongside the steps (an elevator is also available), a floor-to-ceiling

Seven Mile Beach

Sights

Camana Bay
Observation Tower, 1

National Gallery
of the
Cayman Islands, 2

Restaurants

Abacus, 24

Agua, 23

Al La Kebab, 25

Bàcaro, 1

Beach House, 7

Blue by
Eric Ripert, 10

The Brooklyn, 22

Casa 43 Mexican
Kitchen &
Tequila Bar, 12

Chicken!
Chicken!, 18

Cimboco, 26

Coccoloba, 3

Craft Food &
Beverage Co, 27

Eats Cafe, 4

Icoa Fine Foods, 28

Island Naturals, 11

Lone Star
Bar and Grill, 17

Luca, 13

Mizu, 19

Morgan's Seafood
Restaurant, 2

Pani Indian
Kitchen, 21

Ragazzi, 16

Seven, 8

Steak Social, 14

Sunshine Grill, 5

Taikun, 9

Thai Orchid, 29

Tillies, 15

The Waterfront
Urban Diner, 20

Yoshi Sushi, 6

Hotels

The Anchorage, 5

Aqua Bay Club, 2

Beachcomber, 13

Caribbean Club, 15

Christopher
Columbus Condos, 4

Comfort Suites
Seven Mile
Beach, 18

Coral Stone Club
Condos, 12

Discovery
Point Club, 3

Grand Cayman
Marriott Beach
Resort, 17

The Grandview
Condos, 19

Harbour View
Apartments, 20

Kimpton Seafire
Resort & Spa, 6

The Meridian, 14

Palm Heights, 16

Plantana
Condominiums, 7

The Ritz-Carlton
Grand Cayman, 11

Silver Sands, 1

Sunshine Suites
Resort, 9

Villas of
the Galleon, 10

The Westin Grand
Cayman
Seven Mile Beach
Resort & Spa, 8

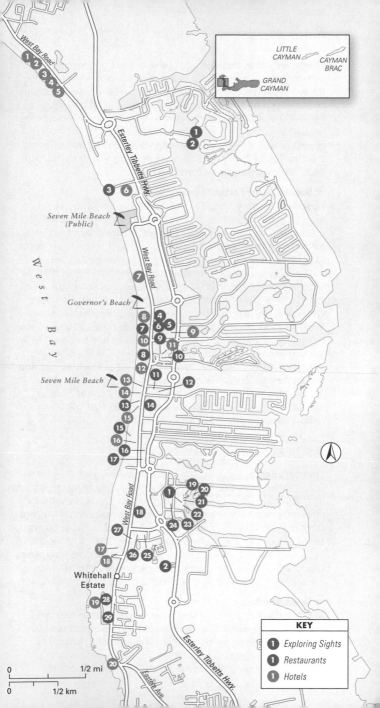

KEY

🔵 *Exploring Sights*

🔴 *Restaurants*

🟤 *Hotels*

mosaic replicates the look and feel of a dive from seabed to surface. Constructed of tiles in 114 different colors, it's one of the world's largest marine-theme mosaics. Benches and lookout points let you take in the views as you ascend. Afterward you can enjoy 500-acre Camana Bay's gardens, waterfront boardwalk, and pedestrian paths lined with shops and restaurants, or frequent live entertainment. ⊠ *Between Seven Mile Beach and North Sound, Camana Bay* ⊹ *2 miles (3 km) north of George Town* ☎ *345/640–3500* ⊕ *www.camanabay.com* 🎫 *Free.*

★ National Gallery of the Cayman Islands

MUSEUM | A worthy nonprofit, this museum displays and promotes Caymanian artists and craftspeople, both established and grassroots. The gallery coordinates first-rate outreach programs for everyone from infants to inmates. It usually mounts six major exhibitions a year, including three large-scale retrospectives or thematic shows, and multimedia installations. Director Natalie Urquhart also brings in international shows that somehow relate to the island, often inviting local artists for stimulating dialogue. The gallery hosts public slide shows, a lunchtime lecture series in conjunction with current exhibits, Art Flix (video presentations on art history, introduced with a short lecture and followed by a discussion led by curators or artists), and a CineClub (movie night). The gallery has also developed an Artist Trail Map with the Department of Tourism and can facilitate studio tours. There's an excellent shop and an Art Café. ⊠ *Esterly Tibbetts Hwy. at Harquail Bypass, Seven Mile Beach* ☎ *345/945–8111* ⊕ *www. nationalgallery.org.ky* 🎫 *Free* ⊗ *Closed Sun.*

 # Beaches

Governor's Beach

BEACH—SIGHT | Located in front of the governor's home, this sandy strip is in the middle of the action, offering incredible snorkeling, strolling, and sunset-watching. With east access and parking out front, you'll find families indulging in beachside picnic or couples sunbathing under the pretty seagrape trees. There's no food here, but a supermarket and restaurants are just across the road. **Amenities:** parking (free), restrooms, water sports. **Best for:** snorkeling, sunset, walking, swimming. ⊠ *West Bay Rd., Seven Mile Beach.*

★ Seven Mile Beach

BEACH—SIGHT | Grand Cayman's west coast is dominated by this famous beach—actually a 5½-mile (10-km) expanse of powdery white sand overseeing lapis water stippled with a rainbow of parasails and kayaks. Free of litter and pesky peddlers, it's an unspoiled (though often crowded) environment. Most of the

Master-planned Camana Bay stretches across 500 acres and is filled with apartments, offices, restaurants, shops, and other businesses.

island's resorts, restaurants, and shopping centers sit along this strip. The public beach toward the north end offers chairs for rent ($10 for the day, including a beverage), a playground, water toys aplenty, beach bars, restrooms, and showers. The best snorkeling is at either end, by the Marriott and Treasure Island or off Cemetery Beach, to the north in West Bay. You can park at the hotels or the malls along West Bay Road, but a dedicated parking lot for day-trippers is at Public Beach. **Amenities:** food and drink; showers; toilets; water sports. **Best for:** partiers; snorkeling. ⊠ *West Bay Rd., Seven Mile Beach.*

Seven Mile Beach Public Beach

BEACH—SIGHT | A busy, white-sand beach with gleaming turquoise waters, this popular stretch of sand just off West Bay Road is peppered with towering, shady palms that throw a welcome shade on the hot sand. Popular with families due to the play park and amenities nearby, you can walk from major hotels or hop in a taxi for a day at this picture-perfect beach. On weekends this vast beach is packed with families hanging out listening to music and having picnics, indulging in water activities, or having a beach-side picnic. **Amenities:** showers; toilets; parking (free). **Best for:** families; water sports; activities. ⊠ *West Bay Rd., Seven Mile Beach.*

Did You Know?

Seven Mile Beach is one of the Caribbean's most beautiful, and it's kept free from litter and pesky peddlers.

🍴 Restaurants

The lion's share of Grand Cayman restaurants is to be found along Seven Mile Beach, where most of the island's resorts are also located. Some are in the strip malls on the east side of West Bay Road, but many are in the resorts themselves.

★ Abacus

$$$$ | **ECLECTIC** | This handsome Camana Bay hangout, once more notable for its stunning decor (witness the smoked glass-and-cast-iron chandeliers) has been transformed into a foodie mecca by executive chef Will O'Hara. Credit his farm-to-table "contemporary Caribbean cuisine" and the solid relationships he's developed with local purveyors, farmers, and fishermen. **Known for:** fab farm-to-table menu; sophisticated space; pork belly specials a standout. $ *Average main: $36* ⊠ *45 Market St., Camana Bay* ☎ *345/623–8282* ⊕ *www.abacus.ky* ⊘ *Closed Sun.*

★ Agua

$$$$ | **ITALIAN** | This quietly hip spot plays up an aquatic theme with indigo glass fixtures, black-and-white photos of bridges and waterfalls, and cobalt-and-white walls that subtly mimic foamy waves. Its young, international chefs emphasize seafood, preparing regional dishes from around the globe with a Caymanian slant, albeit emphasizing Peruvian and Italian specialties from *tiraditos* to *tiramisu*. **Known for:** sensational service; winning wine list and creative cocktails; superlative ceviches. $ *Average main: $31* ⊠ *Camana Bay, 47 Forum La., Seven Mile Beach* ☎ *345/949–2482* ⊕ *www.agua.ky.*

Al La Kebab

$$ | **MIDDLE EASTERN** | Food romps from Malaysia through the Mediterranean to Mexico—spicy chicken tikka, Thai chicken-lemongrass soup, and tzatziki as well as unusual salads and creative sides—at this eatery (subsequent and food trucks). The chef-owner calls it a building-block menu; you can modify the bread and sauce—a dozen varieties, including several curries, peanut satay, jerk mayo, mango *raita* (yogurt, tomatoes, chutney), tahini, teriyaki, garlic cream, even gravy like Mom used to make. **Known for:** fun late-night hangout—open until 4 am weeknights, 3 am weekends; impressive variety of sauces; bargain prices. $ *Average main: $12* ⊠ *Marquee Plaza, West Bay Rd. at Lawrence Blvd., Seven Mile Beach* ☎ *345/943–4343* ⊕ *www.kebab.ky.*

★ Bàcaro

$$$ | **ITALIAN** | Bàcaro (likely derived from Bacchus, Roman god of wine) is the Venetian slang term for a gastropub, dispensing upscale versions of down-home *cichetti* (the city's beloved take on tapas). This dazzling yacht club eatery, boasting gorgeous views of the marina and modish decor (terrific terrace, wonderful black-and-white fishing photos, ropes hung from the ceiling to suggest both keels and sails), delivers on the name's promise thanks to the artistry of Venetian-born head chef–owner Federico Destro, late of Luca. **Known for:** fabulous small plates; comparatively inexpensive and superb-tasting express lunch menus; refined yet chill atmosphere. $ *Average main: $28* ⊠ *Cayman Islands Yacht Club, Yacht Dr., Governor's Creek, Seven Mile Beach* ☏ *345/749–4800* ⊕ *www.bacaro.ky.*

Beach House

$$$ | SEAFOOD | This refined eatery glamorously channels South Beach and Santa Monica, with a sleek black bar, an earthy color scheme, and sparkly ecru curtains dividing dining spaces. Executive chef Sandy Tuason (who apprenticed with the Roux brothers, Daniel Boulud, and David Burke) masterfully adapts Mediterranean and Asian influences to local traditions and ingredients to create a "coastal cuisine" menu that offers mostly small plates and large plates to be shared family-style. **Known for:** superb seafood, especially the charcuterie and salt-baked fish; well-considered if pricey wine list; elegant yet unstuffy atmosphere. $ *Average main: $30* ⊠ *Westin Grand Cayman Seven Mile Beach Resort & Spa, West Bay Rd., Seven Mile Beach* ☏ *345/945–3800* ⊕ *www. westingrandcayman.com* ⊗ *No lunch.*

★ Blue by Eric Ripert

$$$$ | SEAFOOD | Celebrity chef Eric Ripert's trademark ethereal seafood, flawless but not fawning service, swish setting, and soothing, unpretentious sophistication make this one of the Caribbean's finest restaurants. Choose from six- and seven-course tasting menus (with or without wine pairing); there are also trendy "almost raw" and "barely touched" options. **Known for:** stratospheric prices but worth it; stellar service; brilliantly fuses modern French recipes and local ingredients. $ *Average main: $150* ⊠ *Ritz-Carlton Grand Cayman, West Bay Rd., Seven Mile Beach* ☏ *345/943–9000* ⊕ *www.ritzcarlton.com* ⊗ *Closed Sun. and Mon. and Sept.–mid-Nov. No lunch.*

The Brooklyn

$$$ | ECLECTIC | FAMILY | The industrial chic setting of this wildly popular pizza and pasta joint cleverly recalls similar Brooklyn eateries in DUMBO and Williamsburg with natural wood tables for family-style dining, exposed piping, oversize metal lighting fixtures, distressed floors, and silkscreen paintings of musicians like Ray Charles and Diana Ross in Fauvist tones. The food proves equally trendy and appealing. **Known for:** creative pizzas; buzzy atmosphere; smashing cocktails. $ *Average main: $26* ⊠ *The Crescent, Camana Bay* ☎ *345/640–0005* ⊕ *www.thebrooklyncayman.com.*

★ Casa 43 Mexican Kitchen & Tequila Bar

$$ | **MEXICAN** | Mariachi music, sombreros, and intricate Talavera tile work set the tone at this authentic and innovative Mexican eatery tucked away off West Bay Road. Start with the savory ceviches (winners include Caribbean shrimp, Peruvian-style red snapper, and tuna Chino-Latino in soy with sesame, chile, mint, and cilantro). **Known for:** fun, festive staff and atmosphere; tasty tacos and chilaquiles; marvelous margaritas. $ *Average main: $20* ⊠ *43 Canal Point Dr., Seven Mile Beach* ⊹ *Behind Copper Falls Steakhouse* ☎ *345/949–4343* ⊕ *www.casa43.ky* ⊗ *Closed Sun.*

Chicken! Chicken!

$$ | **CARIBBEAN** | **FAMILY** | Devotees would probably award four exclamation points to the marvelously moist chicken, slow-roasted on a hardwood open-hearth rotisserie. Most customers grab takeout, but the decor is appealing for a fast-food joint; the clever interior replicates an old-time Cayman cottage. **Known for:** chicken, chicken, and chicken; fantastic side dishes; low low prices. $ *Average main: $12* ⊠ *West Shore Centre, West Bay Rd., Seven Mile Beach* ☎ *345/945–2290* ⊕ *www.chicken2.com.*

Cimboco

$$ | **ECLECTIC** | **FAMILY** | This animated space celebrates all things fun and Caribbean with pastel walls; cobalt glass fixtures; National Archive photographs and old newspapers about the spot's namesake, *Cimboco,* the first motorized sailing ship built in Cayman (in 1927); and flames dancing up the exhibition kitchen's huge wood-burning oven. Everything from breads (superlative bruschetta and jalapeño corn bread) to ice creams is made from scratch. **Known for:** fun, boldly colored decor; fair prices and hefty servings; clever riffs on staples like pizza with local ingredients. $ *Average main: $19* ⊠ *Marquee Plaza, West Bay Rd. at Harquail Bypass, Seven Mile Beach* ☎ *345/947–2782* ⊕ *www.cimboco.com.*

★ Coccoloba

$$$ | **MEXICAN FUSION** | Despite the deceptively chill vibe at this open-air setup replete with thatching and colorful hand-painted tiles and plates, the fare is haute south-of-the-border. You won't sample finer *chicharrones* (in tangy tequila barbecue sauce), fish tacos, or *elote* (corn off the cob with cotija cheese, cilantro, lime, and chipotle aioli) outside the Yucatan, while the intensely flavored flat-iron steak with mole jus and chimichurri might make even dedicated vegetarians think twice. **Known for:** killer sunset views; innovative Mexican street cuisine; knowledgeable friendly

bartenders. [$] *Average main: $26* ⊠ *Kimpton Seafire Resort & Spa, 60 Tanager Way, Seven Mile Beach* ☎ *345/746–0000, 345/746–4111* ⊕ *www.coccolobacaymanislands.com.*

Craft Food & Beverage Co.

$$$ | ECLECTIC | Arguably Cayman's first true gastropub, Craft impresses with gorgeous postindustrial decor (contrasting warm white exposed brick with gray piping) and contemporary rustic cuisine that defies labels. The kitchen dubs it "familiar food with a twist." The globe-trotting menu changes monthly and the executive chef takes sabbaticals, traveling the world for inspiration. **Known for:** hip but not tragically trendy; awesome cocktail and beer selection; their own house-made condiments are for sale. [$] *Average main: $27* ⊠ *Marquee Plaza, West Bay Rd., Seven Mile Beach* ⊹ *Across from Marriott* ☎ *345/640–0004* ⊕ *www. craftcayman.com.*

Eats Cafe

$$ | ECLECTIC | FAMILY | This busy and eclectic eatery has a vast menu (Cajun to Chinese), including smashing breakfasts and 10 kinds of burgers (fish and veggie versions are available). The decor is dramatic—crimson booths and walls, flat-screen TVs lining the counter, steel pendant lamps, an exhibition kitchen, gigantic flower paintings, and Andy Warhol reproductions. **Known for:** fun buzzy vibe; reasonable prices; extensive "Greek diner" one-from-column-A menu. [$] *Average main: $19* ⊠ *Falls Plaza, West Bay Rd., Seven Mile Beach* ☎ *345/943–3287* ⊕ *www.eats.ky.*

Icoa Fine Foods

$$$ | ECLECTIC | Icoa, the goddess of water, worshipped by the indigenous people of Venezuela's Paria Peninsula, was renowned for her exceptional beauty and alluring perfume. Innovative Dutch chef Jurgen Wevers crafts food that likewise stimulates the senses with cutting-edge cuisine, trotting from Thailand to Tunisia to Tampico, taking center stage. **Known for:** cool Cubist- and Constructivist-inspired artworks; fab Asian street food grazing menu; appealing adjacent wine bar. [$] *Average main: $25* ⊠ *9–11 Seven Mile Shops, West Bay Rd., Seven Mile Beach* ☎ *345/945–1915* ⊕ *www.icoa.ky* ☉ *Closed Sun. No dinner Mon.*

Island Naturals

$ | VEGETARIAN | This café in the heart of Seven Mile beach brings healthy, wholesome, and sustainable ingredients to the streets of Cayman. Everything you see is fresh and chemical-free. **Known for:** all-vegan menu; gluten-free food; smoothies, tea, and coffee. [$] *Average main: $10* ⊠ *Tropic Centre, 12 Earth Close, ground fl., Seven Mile Beach* ☎ *345/945–2252* ⊕ *www.islandnaturals.ky.*

Lone Star Bar and Grill

$$ | **SOUTHWESTERN** | This temple to sports and the cowboy lifestyle serves a Texas-size welcome and portions. If it can be barbecued, deep-fried, jerked, pulled, or nacho-ized, it's probably on the menu. **Known for:** raucous spirited atmosphere; bountiful nightly specials; excellent ribs. $ *Average main: $20 ⊠ 688 W. Bay Rd., Seven Mile Beach* ☎ *345/945–5175* ⊕ *www.lonestarcayman.com.*

★ Luca

$$$$ | **ITALIAN** | At this smart beachfront trattoria, everything has been handpicked: wine wall of more than 3,000 international bottles; Murano glass fixtures; arty blown-up photographs; leather banquettes; and a curving onyx-top bar. Chef Roman Kleinrath presents a more conventional, classic menu than his predecessor but still delights in unorthodox pairings like Hudson Valley foie gras with pickled figs, raspberry balsamic puree, and Port reduction. **Known for:** sleek, sophisticated decor; lovely pastas; fabulous if expensive wine list. $ *Average main: $42 ⊠ Caribbean Club, 871 W. Bay Rd., Seven Mile Beach* ☎ *345/623–4550* ⊕ *luca. ky* ☉ *Closed Mon. in Sept. and Oct. No lunch Sat.*

Mizu

$$$ | **ASIAN** | It's a toss-up as to which is sexier at this pan-Pacific bistro: the sleek decor or the glistening, artfully presented food. The first, courtesy of Hong Kong designer Kitty Chan, is as sensuous as a 21st-century opium den with a back-lit dragon, contemporary Buddhas, glowing granite bar, wildly hued throw pillows, and enormous mirrors. **Known for:** ultrahip decor and staff; huge portions ideal for sharing; surprisingly authentic Asian fare. $ *Average main: $27 ⊠ The Crescent, Camana Bay* ☎ *345/640–0001* ⊕ *www.mizucayman.com.*

★ Morgan's Seafood Restaurant

$$$$ | **ECLECTIC** | Energetic, effervescent Janie Schweiger patrols the front while husband Richard rules the kitchen at this simpatico marina spot where the menu dances just as deftly from Asia dishes like Thai seafood curry to items like chicken schnitzel that highlight the chef's Austrian upbringing. Locals and fishermen literally cruise into the adjacent dock for refueling of all sorts. **Known for:** delightful husband–wife owners; fun peripatetic menu; glorious patio seating overlooking the marina and Governor's Creek. $ *Average main: $39 ⊠ Governor's Creek, Cayman Islands Yacht Club, Seven Mile Beach* ☎ *345/946–7049* ⊕ *www.morgan-scayman.com* ☉ *Closed Tues. and Oct.*

Pani Indian Kitchen

$$$ | **INDIAN** | In every respect, from the decor to the cuisine, Pani is a joyous celebration of street food from around the subcontinent, with haute gloss. The space breathtakingly creates an Indian street bazaar indoors: bamboo-and-burlap awnings, billowing multihue fabric, representations of such deities as Ganesha, a wall of dyed tea bags, and huge brass tandoori urns in the open kitchen. **Known for:** wonderfully flavorful options for vegetarians; fantastic bargain lunch menu; delightful decor including an entire wall of dyed tea bags. $ *Average main: $23* ⊠ *The Crescent, Camana Bay* ☎ *345/640–0007* ⊕ *www.panicayman.com.*

★ Ragazzi

$$$ | **ITALIAN** | **FAMILY** | The name means "good buddies," and this strip-mall jewel percolates with conversation and good strong espresso. The airy space is convivial—blond woods, periwinkle walls and columns, and handsome artworks of beach scenes, sailboats, and palm trees—and the antipasto alone is worth a visit, as are homemade breadsticks and focaccia, carpaccio, and insalata Caprese. **Known for:** reasonable prices by Cayman standards; scrumptious authentic pizzas and pastas; thoughtful wine list showcasing lesser-known regions. $ *Average main: $27* ⊠ *Buckingham Square, West Bay Rd., Seven Mile Beach* ☎ *345/945–3484* ⊕ *www.ragazzi.ky.*

★ Seven

$$$$ | **STEAKHOUSE** | The Ritz-Carlton's all-purpose dining room, which features tall potted palms, soaring ceilings, a black-and-beige color scheme, and twin wine walls bracketing a trendy family-style table, transforms from a bustling breakfast buffet to an elegant evening eatery. Sinatra and Ella keep a sultry beat while the kitchen jazzes standard meat-and-potatoes dishes with inventive seasonings and eye-catching presentations. **Known for:** magnificent steaks; creative sides like lobster-twice-baked mashed potatoes; terrific happy hour cocktail and bar bite bargains. $ *Average main: $53* ⊠ *Ritz-Carlton Grand Cayman, West Bay Rd., Seven Mile Beach* ☎ *345/943–9000* ⊕ *www.ritzcarlton.com.*

Steak Social

$$$$ | **STEAKHOUSE** | A trendy take on the classical steak house can be found in the heart of Seven Mile Beach. The expansive menu dictates bold offerings using the finest cuts of certified Angus beef and fresh seafood. **Known for:** high-quality steaks; sceney atmosphere; great cocktails. $ *Average main: $40* ⊠ *Caribbean Plaza, West Bay Rd., Seven Mile Beach* ☎ *345/333–2333* ⊕ *www. steaksocial.com* ☾ *Closed Sun. No lunch Mon.–Thurs. or Sat.*

Sunshine Grill

$$ | **CARIBBEAN** | **FAMILY** | This cheerful, cherished locals' secret serves haute comfort food—great burgers, wahoo-mushrooms bites, and fabulous fish tacos—that elevates pub grub to an art

Culinary Quality Control

In more than a decade at the helm of New York's Le Bernardin, sometime *Top Chef* panelist Eric Ripert has garnered every gastronomic accolade. Born in Antibes on the French Riviera, Ripert apprenticed at Parisian institution La Tour d'Argent and Joël Robuchon's Jamin, then worked stateside with Jean-Louis Palladin and David Bouley before Le Bernardin reeled him in. He opened his first "name" restaurant, Blue by Eric Ripert, at the Ritz-Carlton Grand Cayman in 2005. Others have since followed.

The Caribbean wasn't on Ripert's radar, as he has told us, but "the resort owner, Michael Ryan, was in New York for dinner at Le Bernardin. He wanted to discuss the Ritz and me opening its signature restaurant. When I came down, he picked me up, put me on a boat to swim at Stingray City, loaded me with champagne, then came straight here to discuss business. ... I loved it, felt confident because of his commitment to quality and service."

The greatest challenge was "the quality of the seafood, which sounds illogical, but most fish here comes frozen from the United States. We visited fishermen, created a network, to get fresh catch regularly. It's the only item the hotel allows cash for,

so [executive chef Frederic Morineau] carries a big wad! We fought passionately for the quality of the seafood, since that's one of my trademarks. And with so few farmers and growers on island ... produce was even more challenging, but we found squash, salad greens, herbs."

"Trying to use what's already here inspires me," says Morineau. "It's cooking in the landscape. I can now get lemongrass, thyme, mint, basil, papaya, mango, callaloo, sweet potatoes, good stew tomatoes, Scotch bonnet, and other peppers. I'm a big advocate of the locally produced Cayman sea salt." He encourages local purveyors, but paramount was persuading management to commit the funds for specialty products worth the price. "We work with a couple of commercial fishing boats that bring huge wahoo, ocean yellowtail, deep-water snapper from as far afield as Mexico. So fresh and so beautiful, a pleasure to work with."

Ripert draws parallels to his Mediterranean upbringing. "It's a different feel and look, of course, as are the cooking ingredients and preparations. But both cultures place great emphasis on food as a key part of their lives and borrow from many heritages. And both cultures know how to relax and enjoy themselves!"

form at bargain prices. Even the chattel-style poolside building, painted a delectable lemon with lime shutters, multihue interior columns, and orange and blueberry accents, whets the appetite. **Known for:** warm family-friendly atmosphere and staff; fantastic affordable dinner specials; one of locals' top choices for burgers. ⑤ *Average main: $20* ⊠ *Sunshine Suites Resort, 1465 Esterley Tibbetts Hwy., Seven Mile Beach* ☎ *345/949–3000, 345/946–5848* ⊕ *www.sunshinesuites.com.*

★ Taikun

$$$ | JAPANESE | FAMILY | Taikun is an archaic Japanese term of esteem, loosely translated as "Supreme Commander." It's an appropriate designation for this sensuous sushi spot, clad in black with crimson and gray accents and dominated by a buzzy communal table. Start with one of the terrific cocktails or indulge in the superlative sake flights, which can be optimally paired with your sushi. **Known for:** simply sensational sushi; attention to detail include grating wasabi at table; refined yet relaxed ambience. ⑤ *Average main: $27* ⊠ *Ritz-Carlton Grand Cayman, West Bay Rd., Seven Mile Beach* ☎ *345/943–9000* ⊕ *www.ritzcarlton.com/ GrandCayman.*

Thai Orchid

$$$ | THAI | East meets West at this elegant eatery, and the combination makes for a tasty meal. The Thai chefs turn out splendid classics like *yum nuer* (sliced chargrilled strip loin tossed with green salad in lime dressing), and seafood lovers can opt for the fresh sushi, and plentiful vegetarian options include curries perfumed with lemongrass. **Known for:** bargain buffets; congenial waitstaff; good selection of vegetarian dishes. ⑤ *Average main: $28* ⊠ *Queen's Court, West Bay Rd., Seven Mile Beach* ☎ *345/949–7955* ⊕ *www.thaiorchid.ky.*

★ Tillies

$$$$ | CARIBBEAN | Classic Caribbean dishes utilize produce from local farms in a homey environment. Great beach views and tropical atmosphere round out the experience. **Known for:** beachside dining; Caribbean food; sceney atmosphere. ⑤ *Average main: $35* ⊠ *Palm Heights, 747 W. Bay Rd., Seven Mile Beach* ☎ *345/949– 3491* ⊕ *www.tillies.ky.*

The Waterfront Urban Diner

$$ | DINER | FAMILY | Ultracontemporary design with industrial elements (exposed piping, raw timber, tugboat salvage) is a counterpoint to the down-home fare at this bustling glorified diner, whose choice seats are on the patio. Comfort food aficionados can launch into the splendid chicken and waffles, meat loaf, and poutine. **Known for:** comfort food like poutine and a killer cinnamon

roll; fun for families; pleasant outdoor seating area. $ *Average main: $19* ✉ *The Crescent, Camana Bay* ☎ *345/640–0002* ⊕ *www.waterfrontcayman.com.*

Yoshi Sushi

$$$ | **JAPANESE** | This modish locals' lair serves superlative sushi. The main room's scarlet cushions, cherry blown-glass pendant lamps, leather-and-bamboo accents, orchids, and maroon walls create an exciting vibe. **Known for:** innovative rolls and sushi "pizzas"; excellent cocktails; cool vibe. $ *Average main: $23* ✉ *Falls Plaza, West Bay Rd., Seven Mile Beach* ☎ *345/943–9674* ⊕ *www.eats.ky/yoshisushi.html.*

Hotels

Most travelers to Grand Cayman choose to stay on one of the resorts or condo complexes along beautiful Seven Mile Beach. Although not all properties have a beachfront location, they are mostly in close proximity to the action and nearby restaurants, nightlife, and shops.

The Anchorage

$$ | **RENTAL** | These two-bedroom condos are cramped compared with otherwise newer compounds, but fully equipped, modernized, scrupulously clean, and—most important—affordable (at least for garden-view apartments). **Pros:** incredible sweeping panoramas from George Town to West Bay from higher units; nice beach and snorkeling; great pool at the edge of the Caribbean. **Cons:** a bit isolated from action; boxy apartments; steep surcharge for oceanview units. $ *Rooms from: $370* ✉ *1989 W. Bay Rd., Seven Mile Beach* ☎ *345/945–4088* ⊕ *www.theanchoragecayman.com* ⇆ *15 units* ⭘ *No meals.*

Aqua Bay Club

$$$$ | **RENTAL** | One of the older condo complexes, ABC is scrupulously maintained, quiet, and affordable. **Pros:** great snorkeling very close to Cemetery Reef; friendly staff; free Wi-Fi and loaner cell phone for local calls. **Cons:** beach can be rocky; no elevator; well-maintained but slightly dowdy. $ *Rooms from: $600* ✉ *West Bay Rd., Seven Mile Beach* ☎ *345/945–4728, 800/618–1229* ⊕ *www.aquabayclub.com* ⇆ *21 units* ⭘ *No meals.*

Beachcomber

$$$$ | **RESORT** | Beachcomber rose phoenix-like post-Ivan as a glam high-rise with 40 spacious two- to four-bedroom condos (roughly 24 in the rental pool). **Pros:** short walk to grocery stores, restaurants; on a great beach; high-tech amenities. **Cons:** no Wi-Fi on beach; pricey; not for those who want to be center of the

Caribbean Club is an upscale condo complex right on Seven Mile Beach.

action. $ *Rooms from: $1025* ✉ *West Bay Rd., Seven Mile Beach* ☎ *345/943–6500* ⊕ *www.beachcomber.ky* ⤶ *40 rooms.*

★ Caribbean Club

$$$$ | RENTAL | This gleaming boutique facility has a striking lobby with aquariums, infinity pool, and contemporary trattoria, Luca. **Pros:** luxurious, high-tech facilities beyond the typical apartment complex; trendy Italian restaurant; service on the beach. **Cons:** poor bedroom reading lights; though families are welcome, they may find it imposing; daily mad dash to claim the free, first-come cabanas. $ *Rooms from: $1256* ✉ *871 W. Bay Rd., Seven Mile Beach* ☎ *345/623–4500, 800/941–1126* ⊕ *www.caribclub.com* ⤶ *37 condos* ⦿ *No meals.*

Christopher Columbus Condos

$$$ | RENTAL | FAMILY | This enduring favorite on the peaceful northern end of Seven Mile Beach is a find for families with two- and three-bedroom condos. **Pros:** excellent snorkeling and fine beach; great value; complimentary Wi-Fi. **Cons:** car needed; often overrun by families during holidays and summer; top floors have difficult access for physically challenged. $ *Rooms from: $440* ✉ *2013 W. Bay Rd., Seven Mile Beach* ☎ *345/945–4354, 866/311–5231* ⊕ *www.christophercolumbuscondos.com* ⤶ *30 condos* ⦿ *No meals.*

Comfort Suites Seven Mile Beach

$ | HOTEL | This no-frills, all-suites hotel has an ideal location, next to the Marriott and near numerous shops, restaurants, and bars.

Pros: affordable; complimentary buffet breakfast and Wi-Fi; fun, young-ish crowd. **Cons:** rooms nearly a block from the beach with no sea views; no balconies; bar closes early. ⑤ *Rooms from: $258* ✉ *22 Piper Way at West Bay Rd., George Town* ☎ *345/945–7300, 844/229–6267* ⊕ *www.caymancomfort.com* ⋑ *108 suites* ⑩ *Free Breakfast.*

Coral Stone Club Condos

$$$$ | **RENTAL** | In the shadow of the Ritz-Carlton, this exclusive enclave still shines by offering understated barefoot luxury, stellar service, and huge three-bedroom condos. **Pros:** large ratio of beach and pool space to guests; walking distance to restaurants and shops; free airport transfers. **Cons:** expensive in high season; Ritz-Carlton guests sometimes wander over to poach beach space; occasionally spotty maintenance in low season. ⑤ *Rooms from: $1025* ✉ *985 W. Bay Rd., Seven Mile Beach* ☎ *345/945–5820, 888/927–2322* ⊕ *www.coralstoneclub.com* ⋑ *30 condos* ⑩ *No meals.*

Discovery Point Club

$$$$ | **RENTAL** | **FAMILY** | This older but upgraded complex of all oceanfront suites sits at the north end of Seven Mile Beach, 6 miles (9½ km) from George Town, with fabulous snorkeling in the protected waters of nearby Cemetery Reef. **Pros:** caring staff; family-friendly; complimentary Internet. **Cons:** car needed; beach entry rocky in spots; no elevator. ⑤ *Rooms from: $675* ✉ *2043 W. Bay Rd., Seven Mile Beach* ☎ *345/945–4724, 866/384–9980* ⊕ *www. discoverypointclub.com* ⋑ *37 condos* ⑩ *No meals.*

Grand Cayman Marriott Beach Resort

$$$$ | **RESORT** | **FAMILY** | The soaring, stylish marble lobby (with exquisite art glass, majestic stingray bas relief sculpture, sets the "Beach House" tone for this bustling property. **Pros:** good snorkeling and water sports; free bike and kayak rentals; convenient to both George Town and Seven Mile Beach. **Cons:** narrowest section of Seven Mile Beach; beach sometimes washes out; pool and bar often noisy late; $50 resort fee. ⑤ *Rooms from: $599* ✉ *389 W. Bay Rd., Seven Mile Beach* ☎ *345/949–0088, 800/223–6388* ⊕ *www.marriottgrandcayman.com* ⋑ *295 rooms* ⑩ *No meals.*

The Grandview Condos

$$$$ | **RENTAL** | **FAMILY** | Grand view, indeed: all 69 two- and three-bedroom units (sadly only 20 are generally in the rental pool) look smack onto the Caribbean and the beach past splendidly maintained gardens. **Pros:** affable helpful staff including wine concierge; free Wi-Fi (when it's available); nice pool and hot tub. **Cons:** the long beach can be rocky; some units a tad worn though meticulously maintained; not all units have strong access to the

Grand Cayman's Best Spas

Whether meditation is your nightly ritual, or kale-infused drinks your daily go-to, or Bikram yoga your new hobby, we all seem to be jumping on the beautifying mind-and-body bandwagon. These are some of the best spas in Grand Cayman.

BEST HOTEL SPAS

Kimpton Seafire Spa. In addition to its range of treatments, the Kimpton spa has steam rooms and a massive co-ed hydrotherapy pool. ✉ *Kimpton Seafire Resort & Spa, 60 Tanager Way Mile Beach* ☎ *345/746–0000* ⊕ *www.seafireresortandspa. com.*

La Prairie Spa at The Ritz-Carlton Grand Cayman. The large spa is one of the island's most luxurious and also has one of the best hotel gyms on Grand Cayman. ✉ *Ritz-Carlton Grand Cayman, West Bay Rd., Seven Mile Beach* ☎ *345/943–9000* ⊕ *www. ritzcarlton.com.*

Hibiscus Spa at the Westin. One of the largest spas on Grand Cayman offers a wide array of treatments and a full workout center. ✉ *Westin Grand Cayman Seven Mile Beach Resort & Spa, West Bay Rd., Seven Mile Beach* ☎ *345/945–3800* ⊕ *www. westingrandcayman.com.*

Botanika Union Spa. The Marriott's new spa takes a holistic approach and uses organic ingredients. ✉ *Grand Cayman Marriott Beach Resort, 389 W. Bay Rd., Seven Mile Beach* ☎ *345/949–0088* ⊕ *www.marriottgrandcayman.com.*

BEST DAY SPAS

Body Works. Body Works is a spa, yoga studio, and retail store dedicated to natural wellness offering a low-key environment catering to those looking for a personal and customized experience. ✉ *Queen's Court Plaza, West Bay Rd., George Town* ☎ *345/945–6485* ⊕ *www. bodyworkscayman.com.*

No. 11 Spa. From bespoke treatments that focus on building mind-body connection to community events designed to empower and educate, No. 11 offers a cozy and all-inclusive environment to the islands' more than 135 nationalities, giving them the knowledge and experience to provide skin care services and advice to all skin types and tonalities. ✉ *115 Printers Way, George Town* ☎ *345/526–6611* ⊕ *www.no11spa.com.*

Touch of Thai. Experience the hospitality and authentic healing arts of Thailand in this beautiful Grand Cayman day spa. At the charming and intimate facility, the friendly Thai staff ensure a luxurious and restorative experience. ✉ *Park Pl., West Bay Rd., Seven Mile Bech* ☎ *345/949–8989* ⊕ *www.touchofthai.ky.*

Covered chaise longues sit on the beach at the Ritz-Carlton Grand Cayman.

free Wi-Fi signal. [$] *Rooms from: $605 ⊠ 95 Snooze La., Seven Mile Beach* ☎ *345/945–4511, 866/977–6766* ⊕ *www.grandview-condos.com* ⤳ *69 condos* ⍾❶ *No meals* ⌖ *5-night minimum high season.*

Harbour View Apartments

$ | RENTAL | This little sunshine-yellow enclave delivers on the name's promise, with smashing views of the leviathan cruise ships hulking off George Town. **Pros:** sweet, helpful owners; great value (free Wi-Fi and local calls); coin-operated laundry on-site. **Cons:** no pool; rocky, small beach (but great snorkeling); dilapidated furnishings. [$] *Rooms from: $130 ⊠ 19 W. Bay Rd., Seven Mile Beach* ☎ *345/949–5681* ⊕ *www.harbourviewapartments.com* ⤳ *12 apartments* ⍾❶ *No meals.*

★ Kimpton Seafire Resort & Spa

$$$$ | RESORT | FAMILY | Everything about the Seafire displays the Kimpton trademark blend of elegance with a touch of funk, artfully adapted to the tropics. **Pros:** sophisticated without pretension; fabulous service; trademark complimentary extras like evening wine tasting. **Cons:** high $60 resort fee; long walk from some rooms to public spaces; not ideal for guests with mobility issues. [$] *Rooms from: $775 ⊠ 60 Tanager Way, Seven Mile Beach* ☎ *345/746–0000, 855/546–7866, 888/246–4412 toll-free reservations* ⊕ *www.seafireresortandspa.com* ⤳ *266 rooms* ⍾❶ *No meals.*

The Meridian

$$$$ | **RENTAL** | The lavish landscaping and neo-Edwardian architecture with gables, Palladian windows, and grillwork balconies set an understated opulent tone that carries over to the interior—curved enclosed patios larger than many apartments, traditional decor favoring hardwood furnishings, four-poster beds, carved-wood chandeliers, and antique maps. **Pros:** restaurants and supermarket right across the street; meticulously maintained; gorgeous beachfront. **Cons:** some find it a little too popular with families; undeniably elegant but extremely pricey; pool and beach can get crowded. ⑤ *Rooms from: $1025* ⊠ *917 W. Bay Rd., Seven Mile Beach* ☎ *345/945–4002* ⊕ *www.meridian.ky* ⤳ *32 condos* ⦿ *No meals.*

★ Palm Heights

$$ | **HOTEL** | The newest and hottest boutique hotel on Seven Mile Beach is trying to give off the vibe of a billionaire best friend rather than a typical Caribbean resort, but it's a refreshing change of pace and lives up to the hype. **Pros:** beautiful design; large pool; all rooms have ocean views. **Cons:** pricey rates; some rooms are small; slow service. ⑤ *Rooms from: $349* ⊠ *747 W. Bay Rd., Seven Mile Beach* ☎ *203/301–1718, 646/809–7256* ⊕ *palmheights. com* ⤳ *53 suites* ⦿ *No meals.*

Plantana Condominiums

$$$ | **RENTAL** | Plantana is exceedingly lush, set on a stunning stretch of sand with smashing views of the leviathan ships lumbering into George Town and permeated with the sounds of surf and birdsong. **Pros:** Wi-Fi and laundry in all units; great service; unique design. **Cons:** some rooms lack a nice view; lack of privacy in the solaria; old building. ⑤ *Rooms from: $475* ⊠ *1293 W. Bay Rd., Seven Mile Beach* ☎ *345/945–4430* ⊕ *www.plantanacayman. com* ⊟ *No credit cards* ⤳ *49 rooms.*

★ The Ritz-Carlton Grand Cayman

$$$$ | **RESORT** | **FAMILY** | This 144-acre, exquisitely manicured resort, offers unparalleled luxury and service infused with a sense of place, with works by local artists and craftspeople. **Pros:** exemplary service; exceptional facilities with complimentary extras; fine beachfront. **Cons:** annoyingly high resort fee; sprawling with a confusing layout; long walk to beach (over an interior bridge) from most rooms. ⑤ *Rooms from: $1179* ⊠ *West Bay Rd., Seven Mile Beach* ☎ *345/943–9000* ⊕ *www.ritzcarlton.com* ⤳ *389 rooms* ⦿ *No meals.*

Silver Sands

$$$$ | **RENTAL** | Silver Sands is an older compound that anchors the quieter northernmost end of Seven Mile Beach, with terrific snorkeling off the spectacular sweep of glittering sand. **Pros:** fabulous views; vaulted ceilings on second floor; spacious units. **Cons:** lengthy minimum stay in winter; units are cramped; not for those who want to be in the center of the action. $ *Rooms from: $595* ⊠ *2131 W. Bay Rd., Seven Mile Beach* ☎ *345/949–3343* ⊕ *www. silversandscayman.com* ⇴ *42 rooms* ⊚I *No meals* ☞ *Min. stay 3 nights summer, 5 in winter.*

Sunshine Suites Resort

$$ | **HOTEL** | **FAMILY** | This friendly, all-suites hotel is an impeccably clean money saver, and though the somewhat boxy but brightly designed rooms lack balconies, patios, or even views, each has a complete kitchen, pillow-top mattress, flat-screen TV, and free Wi-Fi (laptops can be rented). **Pros:** cheerful staff; rocking little restaurant; free access to business center and to nearby World Gym. **Cons:** poor views; not on the beach; annoying $35 resort fee. $ *Rooms from: $364* ⊠ *1465 Esterley Tibbetts Hwy., off West Bay Rd., Seven Mile Beach* ☎ *345/949–3000, 877/786–1110* ⊕ *www. sunshinesuites.com* ⇴ *131 suites* ⊚I *Free Breakfast.*

Villas of the Galleon

$$$$ | **RENTAL** | **FAMILY** | On the beachfront, snuggled between the Ritz-Carlton and Westin, Galleon's villas are just steps away from groceries, restaurants, nightlife, and water sports. **Pros:** affable management; central location with glorious beach; free DSL and local calls. **Cons:** no pool; slightly boxy room configuration; one-bedroom units do not have a washer/dryer. $ *Rooms from: $500* ⊠ *West Bay Rd., Seven Mile Beach* ☎ *345/945–4433, 866/665–4696* ⊕ *www.villasofthegalleon.com* ⇴ *74 condos* ⊚I *No meals.*

★ The Westin Grand Cayman Seven Mile Beach Resort & Spa

$$$$ | **RESORT** | **FAMILY** | The handsomely designed, well-equipped Westin offers something for everyone, from conventioneers to honeymooners to families, not to mention what the hospitality industry calls "location location location." You can walk a perfect beach or luxuriate in a cabana, enjoy the sumptuous spa, sweat in the state-of-the-art fitness club, get wet with a Red Sail Sports branch, dine at the estimable Beach House, lounge in Grand Cayman's largest freshwater pool (with an ocean view to boot), or loll in the suave piano lounge after dark. **Pros:** terrific children's programs; superb beach (the largest resort stretch at 800 feet); better-than-advertised ocean views. **Cons:** occasionally bustling and impersonal when large groups book; daily $50 resort fee; darned expensive if you can't find an online discount. $ *Rooms from: $859* ⊠ *West Bay Rd., Seven Mile Beach* ☎ *345/945–3800, 800/937–8461* ⊕ *www.westingrandcayman.com* ⇴ *347 rooms* ⊚I *No meals.*

Calling All Corsairs

For 11 days in November, Grand Cayman is transformed into a nonstop, fun-filled festival. The annual **Pirates Week Festival** (⊕ *www. piratesweekfestival.com*) is the country's largest celebration, encompassing more than 30 different events including a kids' fun day, float parade, autocross, landing pageant, and underwater treasure hunt. You'll also encounter street dances, five heritage days (where various districts showcase their unique craft and culinary traditions), fireworks, song contests, costume competitions, cardboard-boat regattas, golf tournaments, swim meets, races, and teen music nights.

Everyone gets involved in the high-spirited high jinks (e.g., dive boats stage mock battles and play practical jokes like filling the decks of "rivals" with cornflakes or jam, while swashbucklers "capture" hotel employees and guests). The opening night is an explosion of fireworks and rollicking bands before crowds of thousands in the George Town streets. Later in the week, another highlight is the mock pirate invasion of Hog Sty Bay and the spirited defense of the capital, culminating in the buccaneers' trial and extravagantly costumed street parades with ornate floats.

Most of the major events are free. The music sizzles, and the evening functions feature delicious, affordable local fare (turtle stew, conch, jerk chicken). Given the enormous popularity of the festival, travelers should reserve hotel rooms and rental cars well in advance. Even taxis are scarce for those wanting to attend the farther-flung heritage days. Hotels, shops, and the festival's administrative office do a brisk biz in corsair couture (you can bring your own stuffed parrot and patch, but leave the sword at home).

 ## Nightlife

BARS AND MUSIC CLUBS

The Attic

BARS/PUBS | This chic sports bar has three billiard tables, classic arcade games (Space Invaders, Donkey Kong), air hockey, and large-screen TVs (nab a private booth with its own flat-panel job). Events are daily happy hours, trivia nights, and the Caribbean's reputedly largest Bloody Mary bar on Sunday. Along with sister "O" Bar, it's ground zero for the Wednesday Night Drinking Club. For a $25 initiation (with T-shirt and personalized leather wristband, toga optional) and $10 weekly activity fee, you're shuttled by bus to three different bars, with free shots and drink specials. ⊠ *Queen's Court, 2nd fl., West Bay Rd., Seven Mile Beach* ☎ *345/949–7665, 345/947–5691.*

Backroom

BARS/PUBS | If you blink, you might miss this intimate speakeasy off West Bay Road. however, it offers an air of sophistication reminiscent of the prohibition years. Famous for award-winning craft cocktails and a vast selection of spirits, it's a place to relax in a leather chair. Smokers can peruse the vast cigar humidor offering a diverse selection to suit even the most discerning cigar aficionado. ⊠ *Regency Court, 672 W. Bay Rd., Seven Mile Beach* ☎ *345/947–7666* ⊕ *www.backroomcaymancigars.com.*

★ The Bar at Ave

BARS/PUBS | It's easy to overlook this bar at the entrance to the Kimpton Seafire's main restaurant unless you're waiting for your table, but that would be a mistake. It's not the decor, which is surprisingly sterile despite the handsome driftwood sculpture hanging from the cathedral ceiling. Rather it's the gregarious mixologists who hold court, inventing cocktails on the spot based on your personality and preferences. You can also order dinner from the extensive regular Ave menu, including such standouts as crispy octopus with warm potato and white bean salad or cavatelli with rabbit ragu. ⊠ *Kimpton Seafire, 60 Tanager Way, Seven Mile Beach* ☎ *345/746–4111* ⊕ *www.seafireresortandspa.com.*

Coconut Club

BARS/PUBS | This Caribbean beach bar and popular cocktail lounge draped in white linens sits on the shores of Seven Mile Beach. Hailing from the creators of Tillie's, The Coconut Club offers bar bites and aperitifs with vegan and vegetarian options. Soak up the sun on a lounger out front, shade yourself at the marble shell-clad bar, or wait until night when the DJs spin records on the sand and the locals come out to play. ⊠ *Palm Heights, 747 W. Bay Rd., Seven Mile Beach* ☎ *646/809–7256* ⊕ *palmheights.com/ restaurants/#CoconutClub.*

Coconut Joe's

BARS/PUBS | You can sit at the bar or swing under a century-old poinciana tree and watch the traffic go by. There are murals of apes everywhere, from gorillas doing shots to a baboon in basketball uniform (in keeping with management's facetious suggestion that you attract your server's attention by pounding your chest while screeching and scratching yourself). Friday swings with DJs and free happy hour munchies. Popular for breakfast. ⊠ *West Bay Rd., Seven Mile Beach* ✛ *Across from Comfort Suites and Marriott* ☎ *345/943–5637.*

Deckers

BARS/PUBS | Always bustling and bubbly, Deckers takes its name from the red English double-decker bus that forms the focal point of the main outdoor bar. You can luxuriate indoors on cushy sofas over a chess game and signature blood-orange mojito; hack your way through the 18-hole safari miniature-golf course; find a secluded nook in the garden terrace framed by towering palms, ornate street lamps, and colonial columns; or dance Thursday through Saturday night to pop, reggae, blues, and country courtesy of the Hi-Tide duo. Worthy Carib-Mediterranean fusion cuisine is a bonus (try the Caribbean lobster mac-and-cheese or the coconut shrimp with citrus marmalade and green papaya salad). Tuesday and Friday reel locals in for All-You-Can-Eat Lobster. ⊠ *West Bay Rd., Seven Mile Beach* ☎ *345/945–6600* ⊕ *www.deckers.ky.*

Fidel Murphy's Irish Pub

BARS/PUBS | Thanks to the unusual logo (a stogie-smoking Castro surrounded by shamrocks) and congenial Irish wit and whimsy, you half expect to find Raúl and Gerry Adams harping on U.S. and U.K. policy over a Harp. The Edwardian decor of etched glass, hardwood, and brass is prefabricated (constructed in Ireland, disassembled, and shipped), but everything else is genuine: the warm welcome, the ales and cider on tap, and the proper Irish stew (the kitchen also turns out conch fritters and lamb vindaloo). Sunday means all-you-can-eat extravaganzas (fish-and-chips, carvery) at rock-bottom prices. Trivia nights, happy hours, and live music lure regulars during the week. Weekends welcome live, televised Gaelic soccer, rugby, and hurling, followed by karaoke and *craic* (if you go, you'll learn the definition). ⊠ *Queen's Court, West Bay Rd., Seven Mile Beach* ☎ *345/949–5189* ⊕ *www.fidel-murphys.com.*

Legendz

BARS/PUBS | This sports bar has a clubby, retro feel—Marilyn Monroe and Frank Sinatra photos channel glamour days, while scarlet booths and bubble chandeliers add oomph. Good luck wrestling a spot at the bar for pay-per-view and major sporting events, but 10 TVs, including two 6-by-8-foot screens, broadcast to every corner. Also an entertainment venue, Legendz books local bands, stand-up comics, and island DJs, and serves grilled fare at reasonable prices. ⊠ *Falls Centre, West Bay Rd., Seven Mile Beach* ☎ *345/943–3287* ⊕ *www.eats.ky/legendz.html.*

Lone Star Bar and Grill

BARS/PUBS | Calling itself Cayman's top dive (some might call it a shrine to Texas and alcohol), this bar is defined by its vast sports memorabilia collection, nearly 30 big-screen TVs tuned to

Barefoot Man

H. George Nowak, aka "Barefoot Man," is hardly your ordinary Calypsonian. The blond-haired German-born, self-described "Nashville musical reject" moved from Munich to North Carolina after his mother remarried an Air Force officer. But "the inveterate map lover" dreamed of island life.

He started his island-hopping career in the U.S. Virgin Islands, then Hawaii, then the Bahamas ("the smaller, less populated, the better"), finally settling in the Cayman Islands in 1971.

He was dubbed Barefoot Boy ("since the nicest pair of footwear I owned were my Voit diving flippers") in 1971. While he'll still throw in a country or blues tune, Barefoot came to love the calypso tradition, especially its double entendres and political commentary.

He'll regale you between sets or over beers with colorful anecdotes of island life.

Barefoot sums up his philosophy simply and eloquently in one of his most popular lyrics (add gentle reggae-ish lilt), "I wish I were a captain, Sailin' on the sea. I'd sail out to an island, Take you there with me. I'd throw away the compass, Oh what a dirty scheme. ... Someday I might wake up, realize where I am, dreamin' like some 10-year-old, out in Disneyland, There is no tomorrow when you're living in a dream."

different events, and excellent margaritas. Trivia and Rock 'n' Roll Bingo nights lasso locals. ✉ *686 W. Bay Rd., Seven Mile Beach* ☎ *345/945–5175* ⊕ *www.lonestarcayman.com.*

Stingers Resort and Pool Bar

BARS/PUBS | Tasty, affordable food is served in an appealing setting (check out the stupendous "stinger" mosaic), with cover-free live music and dancing Thursday and Friday. On Wednesday there is an all-you-can-eat Caribbean luau. The band Heat, local legends, sizzles with energetic, emotional calypso, reggae, soca, salsa, and oldies; limbo dancers and fire-eaters keep the temperature rising. If you recoil from audience participation, stay far away. ✉ *Comfort Suites Grand Cayman, West Bay Rd., Seven Mile Beach* ☎ *345/945–3000, 345/916–4402.*

CIGAR AND WINE LOUNGES

Silver Palm Lounge

PIANO BARS/LOUNGES | The Silver Palm drips with cash and cachet, with a model waitstaff and chic clientele. There's an old-fashioned, leather-clad bar and another section that replicates a classic

English country library (perfect for civilized, proper afternoon tea or a pre- or postdinner champagne or single malt). Also on tap: fab cocktails, including specialty martinis (the Silver Palm cosmopolitan is a winner—Ketel One citron, triple sec, a squeeze of fresh lime juice, and a splash of cranberry topped off with Moët champagne); pages of wines by the glass; and an impressive list of cigars, cognacs, and aged rums. ⊠ *Ritz-Carlton Grand Cayman, West Bay Rd., Seven Mile Beach* ☎ *345/943–9000* ⊕ *www.ritzcarlton.com/GrandCayman.*

★ West Indies Wine Company

WINE BARS—NIGHTLIFE | At this ultracontemporary wine store, purchasing tasting cards allows you to sample any of the 80-odd wines and spirits, available by the sip or half or full glass via the argon-enhanced "intelligent dispensing system." Selections traverse a vast canny range of prices, regions, styles, and terroirs. The enterprising owners struck a deal with neighboring restaurants and gourmet shops to provide appetizers or cheese and charcuterie plates, best savored alfresco at the tables in front of the handsome space. Small wonder savvy locals congregate here after work or a movie at the nearby cineplex. ⊠ *Corner of Market St. and the Paseo, Camana Bay* ☎ *345/640–9492* ⊕ *www.wiwc. ky.*

DANCE CLUBS
"O" Bar

DANCE CLUBS | This trendy black-and-crimson, industrial-style dance club has mixed music (live on Saturday), while juggling, flame-throwing bartenders—practically local celebs—flip cocktails every night. It's as close to a stand-and-pose milieu (mainly an under-30 crowd) as you'll find on Cayman. All-night CI$5 cocktails pack them in Friday night. An upper-level private loft is available by reservation. ⊠ *Queen's Court, West Bay Rd., 2nd fl., Seven Mile Beach* ☎ *345/943–6227, 345/916–0676* ⊙ *Closed Sun.*

🎭 Performing Arts

Harquail Theatre

ARTS CENTERS | This state-of-the-art facility seats 330 for theatrical performances, concerts, dance recitals, fashion shows, beauty pageants, art exhibits, and poetry readings sponsored by the Cayman National Cultural Foundation. ⊠ *17 Harquail Dr., Seven Mile Beach* ☎ *345/949–5477* ⊕ *www.artscayman.org/harquail-theatre.*

Preserving Caymans Cultural Heritage

Several worthy organizations are dedicated to keeping Caymanian traditions alive, including the National Trust of the Cayman Islands, which restores historic buildings and offers craft demonstrations and talks. The Cayman National Cultural Foundation mounts storytelling, musical, dance, and theatrical presentations, as well as readings and art exhibits that respect the "old ways" while seeking new forms of expression. The National Gallery also seeks to ensure vibrant vital world-class artistic development.

Respected local artist Chris Christian (who curates the Ritz-Carlton Gallery exhibits), cofounded **Cayman Traditional Arts** (✉ *CTA, 60 W. Church St., West Bay,* ☎ *345/946–0117* ⊕ *artcayman. blogspot.com*), which offers interactive classes for children and adults interested in learning authentic Caymanian arts, crafts, and recipes: thatch weaving, kite making, gig making and spinning, rope making, and an old-style cookout on the wood-burning oven called a caboose are just some of the topics. The network of freelance artisans has practiced these traditional crafts and customs their entire lives, often handed down over several generations, and represent the best in their disciplines. You really get hands-on in CTA's "living museum" headquarters, a 1917 mauve-and-mint wattle-and-daub cottage with ironwood posts that also doubles as a studio for Chris and Carly Jackson.

🛍 Shopping

ART GALLERIES
Ritz-Carlton Gallery

ART GALLERIES | This gallery more than fulfilled one of the resort's conditions upon securing rights to build, which was to commission local arts and artisans to help decorate the public spaces. The corridor-cum-bridge spanning West Bay Road became a gallery where Chris Christian of Cayman Traditional Arts curates quarterly exhibitions of Cayman's finest (there are also theme shows devoted to photography and local kids' art). Each piece is for sale; CTA or the hotel will mediate in the negotiations between artist and buyer at a favorable commission. ✉ *Ritz-Carlton Grand Cayman, West Bay Rd., Seven Mile Beach* ☎ *345/943–9000, 345/926–0119.*

BOOKS
Books & Books
BOOKS/STATIONERY | **FAMILY** | The Miami independent bookseller operates this outlet in Grand Cayman. Regular events include author readings and "Floetry," when poets and performers express themselves at the open mike. Two entire rooms are devoted to kids with toys, educational games, and books from toddler to YA; twice-weekly story and craft time keep them occupied while parents browse. Starbucks is also next door. ⊠ *45 Market St., Camana Bay* ☎ *345/640–2665* ⊕ *shop.booksandbooks. com/grandcayman.*

FOOD
Foster's
FOOD/CANDY | Foster's is the biggest supermarket chain on the island, with seven stores scattered across Grand Cayman. The stores offer a wide selection of specialty, organic, local, name-brand, and global products at an everyday, affordable prices (for Cayman anyway). The Camana Bay location has the largest deli-style café on island, offering an extensive selection of daily offerings for breakfast, lunch, and dinner. ⊠ *Camana Bay, Solaris Ave., Seven Mile Beach* ☎ *345/945–4748* ⊕ *fosters.ky.*

SHOPPING CENTERS
Galleria Plaza
SHOPPING CENTERS/MALLS | Nicknamed Blue Plaza for its azure hue, Galleria Plaza features several galleries and exotic home-accessories stores dealing in Oriental rugs or Indonesian furnishings, as well as more moderate souvenir shops hawking T-shirts and swimwear. ⊠ *West Bay Rd., Seven Mile Beach.*

The Strand Shopping Centre
SHOPPING CENTERS/MALLS | This mall has branches of Tortuga Rum and Blackbeard's Liquor, Polo Ralph Lauren and another Kirk Freeport (this location is particularly noteworthy for china and crystal, from Kosta Boda to Baccarat, as well as a second La Parfumerie). You'll also find ATMs galore so you can withdraw cash. ⊠ *West Bay Rd., Seven Mile Beach.*

West Shore Shopping Centre
SHOPPING CENTERS/MALLS | Dubbed Pink Plaza for reasons that become obvious upon approach, West Shore offers upscale boutiques and galleries (tenants range from Chicken Chicken to 'Treasure Tee's). ⊠ *West Bay Rd., Seven Mile Beach.*

Activities

DIVING
Ambassador Divers

SCUBA DIVING | This on-call (around the clock), guided scuba-diving operation offers trips for two to eight persons. Co-owner Jason Washington's favorite spots include sites on the West Side and South and North Wall. Ambassador offers three boats: a 28-foot custom Parker (maximum six divers), a 46-foot completely custom overhauled boat, and a 26-footer primarily for snorkeling. Divers can be picked up from their lodgings. A two-tank boat dive is $115. ⊠ *Palm Heights Hotel, 747 W. Bay Rd., Seven Mile Beach* ☎ *345/949–4530, 844/507–0441 toll-free* ⊕ *www.ambassadordivers.com.*

★ Indigo Divers

SCUBA DIVING | This full-service, mobile PADI teaching facility specializes in exclusive guided dives from its 28-foot Sea Ray Bow Rider or 32-foot Stamas, the *Cats Meow* and the *Cats Whiskers*. Comfort and safety are paramount. Luxury transfers are included, and the boat is stocked with goodies like fresh fruit and home-made cookies. Captain Chris Alpers has impeccable credentials: a licensed U.S. Coast Guard captain, PADI master scuba diver trainer, and Cayman Islands Marine Park officer. Katie Alpers specializes in wreck, DPV, dry suit, boat, and deep diving, but her primary role is videographer. She edits superlative DVDs of the adventures with music and titles. They guarantee a maximum of six divers. The individual attention is pricier; the larger the group, the more you save. ⊠ *Seven Mile Beach* ☎ *345/946–7279, 345/525–3932* ⊕ *www.indigodivers.com.*

Red Sail Sports

SCUBA DIVING | **FAMILY** | Daily trips leave from most major hotels, and dives are often run as guided tours, good for beginners. If you're experienced and your air lasts long, ask the captain if you must come up with the group (when the first person runs low on air). Kids' options (ages 5 to 15) include SASY and Bubblemakers. The company also operates Stingray City tours, dinner and sunset sails, and water sports from Wave Runners to windsurfing. ☎ *345/949–8745, 345/623–5965, 877/506–6368* ⊕ *www.redsailcayman.com.*

GOLF
North Sound Golf Club

GOLF | Formerly the Links at Safehaven, this is Cayman's only 18-hole golf course and infamous among duffers for its strong wind gusts. Roy Case factored the wind into his design, which incorporates lots of looming water and sand bunkers. The hand-some setting features many mature mahogany and silver thatch trees where iguana lurk. Wear shorts at least 14 inches long (15 inches for women) and collared shirts. Greens fees change seasonally, and there are twilight and walking discounts (though carts are recommended), a fine pro shop, and an open-air bar with large-screen TVs. ✉ *557 Safehaven Dr., Seven Mile Beach ✛ Off West Bay Rd.* ☎ *345/947-4653* ⊕ *www.northsoundclub.com* ✉ *$175 for 18 holes, $110 for 9 holes, including cart; twilight rates* ⅄ *18 holes, 6605 yards, par 71.*

Ritz-Carlton Golf Club
GOLF | Designed by Greg Norman in 2006 and built on undulating terrain near mangroves, this lovely course, formerly dubbed Blue Tip, is now open to non-Ritz-Carlton guests as well. Five of the holes are par-4s, and two are par-5s, including a 600-yarder, so there is plenty of muscle to the layout. Abundant water hazards, tricky winds, and sudden shifts in elevation challenge most duffers. No jeans are allowed, and you must wear collared golf shirts. Club rentals are available at the golf shop. ✉ *Ritz-Carlton Grand Cayman, West Bay Rd., Seven Mile Beach* ☎ *345/943–9000, 345/815–6500* ⊕ *www.ritzcarlton.com* ✉ *$195 for 18 holes, $125 for 9 holes; twilight discounts* ⅄ *9 holes, 3515 yards, par 36.*

SAILING
Sail Cayman
SAILING | Neil Galway, an experienced RYA Yacht Master, runs Sail Cayman, offering 30-foot Gemini RIB ecotours and two seawor-thy sailboats including the 47-foot Beneteau, *Splendour in the Wind,* for full-day or half-day private sailing or snorkeling. Though not bareboating, it is hands-on: you can crew and even captain if you enjoy sailing. Neil personalizes the cruise to suit any family or group, including Bio Bay night snorkeling, accommodating a maximum of 12–15 passengers. A half day runs $800, a full day $1,400 and up, which includes a deli-style lunch; if you have a large group, it's little more than the price for crowded excursions with twice as many strangers. ✉ *Yacht Club docks B-48, D-15, and D-17, Seven Mile Beach* ☎ *345/916–4333* ⊕ *www.sailcayman.com.*

SNORKELING
Captain Marvin's
SNORKELING | Multistop North Sound snorkeling trips, as well as fishing charters and land tours, are offered by the indomitable, irrepressible Captain Marvin. One of the first regular Stingray City operators (in business since 1951), he is still going strong in his nineties, though he rarely takes the boats out himself. Full-day trips include lunch and conch dives November–April, when the

crew prepares marinated conch as the appetizer; other excursions include the Crystal Caves. The half day (three hours) tour is the best deal; though large groups can be a drawback. Reservations can be made only from 10 to 3 on weekdays or via the website. Cash payments usually receive a discount. ⊠ *Cayman Islands Yacht Club, Seven Mile Beach* ☎ *345/945–7306, 345/945–6975* ⊕ *www.captainmarvins.com.*

Fantasea Tours

SNORKELING | **FAMILY** | Captain Dexter Ebanks runs tours on his 38-foot trimaran, *Don't Even Ask,* usually departing from the Cayman Islands Yacht Club ($40 including transfers, $30 children under 12). Tours are not too crowded (22 people max) and Ebanks is particularly helpful with first-timers. Like many captains, he has pet names for the rays (ask him to find Lucy, whom he "adopted") and rattles off factoids during an entertaining, nonstop narration. It's a laid-back trip, with Bob Marley and Norah Jones playing, fresh fruit and rum punch on tap. ⊠ *West Bay Rd., Seven Mile Beach* ☎ *345/916–0754* ⊕ *www.dexters-fantaseatours.com.*

SQUASH AND TENNIS

The Courts

SQUASH/RACQUETBALL/PADDLEBALL | Originally a collaboration between Ritz-Carlton Grand Cayman and tennis coach Nick Bollettieri (former mentor of Andre Agassi, Monica Seles, Maria Sharapova, Jim Courier, and the Williams sisters at his legendary Florida academy), the club offers three French-style red clay courts and two Wimbledon-worthy grass courts. The now-independent pros give private lessons ($125); court rental is $40 per hour. ⊠ *West Bay Rd., Seven Mile Beach* ☎ *345/943–9000.*

Chapter 5

WEST BAY

Updated by
Monica Walton

⊙ Sights   🍴 Restaurants   🛏 Hotels   🛍 Shopping   🍸 Nightlife
★★★☆☆   ★★★★☆   ★★☆☆☆   ★★★☆☆   ★★★☆☆

NEIGHBORHOOD SNAPSHOT

TOP EXPERIENCES

■ **Kitesurfing at Barkers:** Kitesurf and Windsurf Cayman are a short drive north of Seven Mile Beach.

■ **Shore diving at Macabuca bar:** Turtle reef is a popular spot for divers and snorkelers.

■ **Snorkeling with turtles:** Grab your snorkel and fins, and jump in with wild green sea turtles at the Cayman Turtle Centre.

■ **Horseback riding on the beach:** Several companies take riders on tours along secluded Barkers Beach.

■ **Indulge in local food:** You'll find a collection of casual Caribbean eateries scattered across West Bay.

GETTING HERE

West Bay lies just to the north of Seven Mile Beach and is home to a slew of winding roads that make it an easy place to get lost. The WB1 (with a yellow circle) and 3 (purple circle) buses run frequently along West Bay Road. The Cayman Turtle Centre also has a free shuttle to and from hotels and the park.

PLANNING YOUR TIME

You have your choice here. Spend a morning at the Cayman Turtle Centre, eat local food at Heritage Kitchen, try shore diving at Macabuca, go horseback riding on Barkers Beach. If you are driving, stop in at Hell for a picture. Want to do nothing and just soak up the rays? Public beach makes it easy for beach bums looking to laze around.

QUICK BITES

■ **Heritage Kitchen.** Expect lengthy queues because both tourists and locals flock here for whole fried snapper and coconut mahi-mahi. ⊠ *Just off Boggy Sand Rd.* ☎ *345/916–0444* ⊕ *www.heritagekitchencayman.com.*

■ **Macabuca Oceanside Tiki Bar.** Transforms from a casual tiki bar for divers by day to an exquisite high-end restaurant at night. One must try: the homemade ice-cream sandwich. ⊠ *857 N.W. Point Rd.* ☎ *345/945–5217* ⊕ *www.cracked-conch.com.ky.*

■ **Vivo.** Catering to the gluten-free and vegan crowd, this easygoing café serves up ecofriendly dishes like their famed lionfish burger. ⊠ *Lighthouse Point Resort, 571 N.W. Point Rd.* ☎ *345/749–8486* ⊕ *www.vivo.ky.*

With crystalline waters and beaches that quite literally sparkle, the district of West Bay is packed with popular attractions and delightful Cayman cottages, and the whole area emits that "islandy feel" you so seldom find anywhere, and here visitors are treated as one of the locals.

Life in West Bay ambles at a slower speed than on busier Seven Mile Beach. Perched on the west side of Grand Cayman, giant casuarina trees guard white-sand bays like Cemetery Beach and Public Beach. Brightly colored shacks sit atop baby soft sand, shading beach bums and running children alike. Just down a winding road, you'll find one of the region's most popular attractions: the so-called Hell, a collection of short, black, limestone formations roughly the size of a football field that only looks hellish. Riding horseback in the tranquil waters of Barkers Beach is one for the bucket list, and if the weather is breezy enough, you can kite-board in the bay here. The warm, flat waters and expansive open space offers first-timers the perfect learning environment. After horseback riding at Barkers, head to another of the island's most popular attractions, the Cayman Islands Turtle Centre, a playground for green sea turtles, exotic birds, and marine life. Spend the rest of the day pottering around the man-made beach, eating at one of the local restaurants before catching the sunset. If you're lucky, you may even see the elusive green flash. This is primarily a residential area, and there aren't many hotels on this part of Grand Cayman, meaning it's quieter and easier to escape. But many tourists come to several popular restaurants that are located here.

Sights

Cayman Turtle Centre
AMUSEMENT PARK/WATER PARK | FAMILY | Cayman's premier attraction has been transformed into a marine theme park with souvenir shops and restaurants. The turtles remain a central attraction, and you can tour ponds in the original breeding and research facility with thousands in various stages of growth, some up to 600 pounds and more than 70 years old. Four areas—three aquatic and one dry—cover 23 acres; different-color bracelets determine access (the steep all-area admission includes snorkeling gear and

In addition to being the island's most popular tourist attraction, the Cayman Turtle Centre breeds green sea turtles for release.

waterslides). The park helps promote conservation, encouraging interaction (a tidal pool houses invertebrates such as starfish and crabs) and observation. Animal Program events include Keeper Talks, where you might feed birds or iguanas, and biologists' conservation programs. The freshwater **Breaker's Lagoon,** replete with cascades plunging over moss-carpeted rocks, evokes Cayman Brac. The saltwater **Boatswain's Lagoon,** replicating all the Cayman Islands and the Trench, teems with 14,000 denizens of the deep milling about a cannily designed synthetic reef. (You can snorkel here—lessons and guided tours are available.) Both lagoons have underwater 4-inch-thick acrylic panels that look directly into **Predator Reef,** home to six brown sharks, four nurse sharks, and other predatory fish such as tarpons, eels, and jacks, which can also be viewed from terra (or "terror," as one guide jokes) firma. Look for feeding times. The free-flight **Aviary**, designed by consultants from Disney's Animal Kingdom, is a riot of color and noise with feathered friends representing the entire Caribbean basin; it doubles as a rehabilitation center for Cayman Wildlife and Rescue. A winding interpretive nature trail culminates in the **Blue Hole**, a collapsed cave once filled with water. Audio tours are available with different focuses, from butterflies to bush medicine. The last stop is the living museum, **Cayman Street**, with facades duplicating vernacular architecture. ⊠ 786 N.W. Point Rd., West Bay ☎ 345/949–3894 ⊕ www.turtle.ky ☜ $45 all-access, $18 Turtle Farm only.

Turtles and Cats

Blessed with arguably the world's largest turtle nesting grounds, Cayman developed into the center of the Caribbean turtle industry for nearly two centuries. English settlers on Jamaica became particularly proficient turtlers. Once they hunted the population into near-extinction by the early 1800s, Caymanians went to sea for months, trapping and supplying turtles from Cuba and Nicaragua well into the 20th century. Even today roughly 20 locals are licensed to catch four turtles annually, and the Cayman Turtle Centre (an environmentally sensitive "working" part of the marine theme park formerly known as Boatswain's Beach) supplies the local market with farm-raised meat.

Turtling led indirectly to one of the proud Caymanian contributions to shipbuilding, the catboat. The design of this basic sailboat (not a catamaran) is usually credited to Cayman Brac's Daniel Jervis circa 1904, though Cape Cod and Chesapeake Bay boaters debate the origin. He decided to bring the stern to a sharp point, similar to New England/Canadian whalers and peapods, placing the mast in the bow. Supposedly, the shape permitted quicker course reversal and less drag, while the lack of keel depth facilitated beaching the boat. Ballast provided stability, and only a yoke was used to steer the rudder.

The Cayman Catboat Club holds several annual regattas as well as free rides during special events, including Pirates Week.

Hell

NATURE SITE | FAMILY | Quite literally the tourist trap from Hell, especially when overrun by cruise-ship passengers, this attraction does offer free admission, fun photo ops, and sublime surrealism. Its name refers to the quarter-acre of menacing shards of charred brimstone thrusting up like vengeful spirits (actually blackened and "sculpted" by acid-secreting algae and fungi over millennia). The eerie lunarscape is now cordoned off, but you can prove you had a helluva time by taking a photo from the observation deck. The attractions are the small post office and a gift shop where you can get cards and letters postmarked from Hell, not to mention wonderfully silly postcards titled "When Hell Freezes Over" (depicting bathing beauties on the beach), "The Devil Made Me Do It" bumper stickers, Scotch bonnet–based Hell sauce, and "The coolest shop in Hell" T-shirts. Ivan Farrington, the owner of the Devil's Hang-Out store, cavorts in a devil's costume (horn, cape, and tails), regaling you with demonically bad jokes. ⊠ *Hell Rd., West Bay* ☎ *345/949–3358* ☜ *Free.*

Beaches

Barkers

BEACH—SIGHT | Secluded, spectacular beaches are accessed via a dirt road just past Papagallo restaurant. There are no facilities (that's the point!), but some palms offer shade. Unfortunately, the shallow water and rocky bottom discourage swimming, and it can be cluttered at times with seaweed and debris. You may also encounter wild chickens (their forebears released by owners fleeing Hurricane Ivan in 2004). Kitesurfers occasionally come here for the gusts; it's also popular for horseback riding. **Amenities:** none. **Best for:** solitude; walking; windsurfing. ⊠ *Conch Point Rd., Barkers, West Bay.*

Cemetery Beach

BEACH—SIGHT | A narrow, sandy driveway takes you past the small cemetery to a perfect strand just past the northern end of Seven Mile Beach. The dock here is primarily used by dive boats during winter storms. You can walk in either direction. The sand is talcum-soft and clean, the water calm and clear (though local surfers take advantage of occasional small reef breaks), and the bottom somewhat rocky and dotted with sea urchins, so wear reef shoes if wading. You'll definitely find fewer crowds. **Amenities:** none. **Best for:** snorkeling; solitude; surfing. ⊠ *West Bay Rd., Seven Mile Beach.*

West Bay Public Beach

BEACH—SIGHT | Famous for its picturesque palm trees and aquamarine waters, West Bay's public beach is a popular tourist stop. With parking and picnic areas, it's a great choice for a day of beach-bumming. Zip around on a Jet Ski, or take some snaps just chilling on your lounger. This stunning crescent-shape beach offers incredible snorkeling and sunset views. Take a stroll out to the water's edge, where you can gaze at the brightly colored coral, or strap on your snorkel and expect to see blue tangs and other species of fish. **Amenities:** food and drink; parking (free); toilets; water sports. **Best for:** snorkeling; sunset; swimming; walking. ⊠ *2089 West Bay Rd., West Bay.*

🍴 Restaurants

There are fewer restaurant choices in West Bay, but there are some spots that are worth the trip. Be sure to have good driving directions when heading out into this area.

West Bay

LITTLE CAYMAN
CAYMAN BRAC
GRAND CAYMAN

Caribbean Sea

Head of Barkers

Barkers

Hell Road

West Bay

KEY

● 1	Exploring Sights
● 1	Restaurants
● 1	Hotels

Cemetery Beach

West Bay Road

Esterley Tibbetts Hwy.

0   1/2 mi
0   1/2 km

West Bay Public Beach

West Bay

West Bay Road

Whitehall Estate

Sights

Cayman Turtle Centre, **1**

Hell, **2**

Restaurants

Alfresco, **4**

Calypso Grill, **8**

The Cracked Conch, **2**

Heritage Kitchen, **6**

Liberty's, **3**

Ristorante Pappagallo, **7**

VIVO Cafe and Restaurant, **1**

West Bay Diner, **5**

Hotels

Lighthouse Point Resort, **1**

Shangri-La B&B, **2**

A traditional Cayman cottage at Boatswain's Beach

Alfresco

$$$ | **CARIBBEAN** | This ultrafriendly locals' insider spot (though celeb sightings have run from Shaq to Sly Stallone), straddling the unofficial "border" between Seven Mile Beach and West Bay, resembles a little neighborhood diner transported to the ocean. Enjoy equally fresh sea breezes and food on the waterfront wood deck under one of the mismatched umbrellas. **Known for:** breezy patio overlooking Caribbean; delicious local food; warm welcome. ⑤ *Average main: $25* ⊠ *53 Town Hall Rd., West Bay* ☎ *345/947–2525* ⊕ *www.alfrescobythesea.com.*

Calypso Grill

$$$$ | **ECLECTIC** | Shack-chic describes this inviting split-level eatery; the interior feels like a Caribbean painting, while the outdoor deck, with a view of frigate birds circling fishing boats, is a Winslow Homer. The menu emphasizes fish hauled in at the adjacent dock, fresh and rarely overcooked. **Known for:** wonderfully colorful decor; entrancing views of North Sound; superb seafood. ⑤ *Average main: $44* ⊠ *Morgan's Harbour, West Bay* ☎ *345/949–3948* ⊕ *www.calypsogrillcayman.com* ⊘ *Closed Mon.*

The Cracked Conch

$$$$ | **ECLECTIC** | This island institution effortlessly blends upscale and down-home as the capable chefs reinvent familiar dishes to create such delectables as crispy calamari with cardamom-marinated carrots, saffron aioli, chili jam, and chipotle sauce. The interior gleams from the elaborate light-and-water sculpture at the gorgeous mosaic-and-mahogany entrance Bubble Bar to the

plush booths with subtly embedded lighting. **Known for:** sensational views; creative dishes fusing local ingredients and Continental classics; lively waterside bar section with specials; Sunday brunch. $ *Average main: $45 ⊠ 857 N.W. Point Rd., West Bay* ☎ *345/945–5217 ⊕ www.crackedconch.com.ky ⊗ Closed Sept. No lunch June–Nov.*

Heritage Kitchen

$$ | CARIBBEAN | West Bay's popular family-run restaurant serves up legendary raconteur Tunny Powell's fish tea, coconut grouper, barbecue ribs, and fish fry—with a generous portion of local lore and sterling sea views. The colorfully painted, gingerbread-trim lean-to is easy to miss from the main road, so look for it when you're in the area. Just go early because it's only open until 6 pm. **Known for:** to-die-for Cayman classics such as fish tea; terrific place for island gossip and lore; lovely sea views. $ *Average main: $15 ⊠ Heritage Sq., Just off Boggy Sand Rd., West Bay* ☎ *345/916–0444 ⊕ www.heritagekitchencayman.com ⊗ Closed Mon. and Tues. No dinner.*

Liberty's

$$ | CARIBBEAN | Just follow the boisterous laughter and pulsating Caribbean tunes to this hard-to-find mint-green Caymanian cottage, where you feel like you've been invited to a family reunion. The Sunday Caribbean buffet attracts hordes of hungry church goers (call ahead to ensure they're open that week), but every day offers authentic turtle steak, oxtail, jerk, and delectable fried snapper with sassy salsas that liberate your taste buds from the humdrum. **Known for:** extravagant Sunday buffet; good authentic local food; warm staff and clientele. $ *Average main: $18 ⊠ 140 Reverend Blackman Rd., West Bay* ☎ *345/949–3226.*

Ristorante Pappagallo

$$$$ | ITALIAN | Pappagallo, Italian for "parrot," hauntingly perches on the edge of a lagoon in a 14-acre bird sanctuary. Inside, riotously colored macaws, cockatoos, and parrots perch on swings behind plate glass, but Italian-born Chef Alex Menegon's food is definitely not for the birds, especially his sublime risotto, pastas, and oh-so-yummy osso buco. **Known for:** marvelously romantic "jungle" setting; delectable Italian fare; smart food and wine/cocktail pairings. $ *Average main: $40 ⊠ Barkers, 444B Conch Point Rd., West Bay* ☎ *345/949–1119 ⊕ www.pappagallo.ky ⊗ No lunch.*

VIVO Cafe and Restaurant

$$ | VEGETARIAN | This peaceful waterfront restaurant offers one of the best views in Cayman. You may be wowed by the gluten-free yet delicious dishes—all Caribbean inspired, of course. **Known for:** mostly vegetarian menu, along with some seafood; many

Food Fêtes

Gastronomy is big business on Grand Cayman, as upmarket eateries bank on the tourist dollar. Increasingly popular culinary events introduce visitors to local culture while beefing up biz, especially off-season. Celeb chef Eric Ripert debuted "Caribbean Rundown" weekend in 2007 at his Blue by Eric Ripert in the Ritz-Carlton, including cooking classes, fishing trips, and gala dinners, *Top Chef* competitor Dale Levitzki in tow. It was such a success that *Food & Wine* cosponsors the subsequent editions—now called Cayman Cookout—every January, with even more top toques stirring the broth: a recipe for success in this case. Both fests benefit local charities. February's "A Taste of Cayman" has titillated taste buds for more than two decades, thanks to more than 30 participating restaurants, raffles, entertainment, and cook-offs.

vegan and gluten-free dishes; amazing views. $ *Average main: $18* ⊠ *Lighthouse Point Resort, 571 N.W. Point Rd., West Bay* ☎ *345/749–8486* ⊕ *www.vivo.ky.*

West Bay Diner
$$ | CARIBBEAN | Rustic Caribbean meets casual American at this roadside eatery in West Bay. The spot is locally famous for its quick bites, breakfasts, and a limited menu of staple dishes. **Known for:** Caribbean-American food; casual atmosphere and food; breakfast. $ *Average main: $13* ⊠ *32 Town Hall Rd., West Bay* ☎ *345/946–8000.*

Hotels

For those who want to be out of the thick of things, yet still fairly close to Seven Mile Beach, there are a handful of resorts and condo rentals available in West Bay. Some of these even have waterfront locations, though they are fronted by ironshore rather than a sandy white beach.

★ Lighthouse Point Resort
$$$$ | RESORT | Scuba operator DiveTech's stunning ecodevelopment (motto "living lightly on the planet") features sustainable wood interiors and recycled concrete, a gray-water system, energy-saving appliances and lights, and Cayman's first wind turbine generator. **Pros:** ecofriendly; fantastic shore diving (and state-of-the-art dive shop); superb restaurant on-site. **Cons:** no real beach; car necessary; a bit difficult for physically challenged to

Lighthouse Point is the ultimate dive resort.

navigate. $ *Rooms from: $325* ✉ *571 N.W. Point Rd., West Bay* ☎ *345/949–1700, 877/946–5658* ⊕ *www.lighthousepointresort. com* ⇥ *9 apartments* ⦿| *No meals.*

Shangri-La B&B

$ | **B&B/INN** | Understated good taste informs every aspect of this lavish lakeside retreat, from the waterfall pool and hot tub to a screened-in patio overlooking the bird-filled lagoon to the carved hardwood furnishings, tatted linens, and ornately embroidered pillows, and scrumptious breakfasts (to-die-for bread-and-butter pudding and sticky toffee souffle). **Pros:** elegant decor; DVD players and Wi-Fi included; rental bikes free. **Cons:** rental car necessary; not on the beach; hard to find. $ *Rooms from: $260* ✉ *1 Sticky Toffee La., West Bay* ☎ *345/526–1170* ⊕ *www.shangrilabandb.com* ⇥ *7 rooms, 1 apartment* ⦿| *Free Breakfast.*

Nightlife

BARS AND MUSIC CLUBS
★ Macabuca Oceanside Tiki Bar

BARS/PUBS | This classic beach bar has a huge deck over the water, thatched roof, amazing mosaic murals of waves, spectacular sunsets (and sunset-color libations), and tiki torches illuminating the reef fish come evening. *Macabuca* means "What does it matter?" in the indigenous Antillean Taíno language, perfectly encapsulating the mellow vibe. Big-screen TVs, live bands and DJs on weekends, excellent pub grub, and daily specials (CI$9 jerk dishes weekends; Monday all-night happy hour, DJ, and CI$17 all-you-can-eat barbecue) lure everyone from well-heeled loafers to barefoot bodysurfers animatedly discussing current events and dive currents in a Babel of tongues. ✉ *857 N.W. Point Rd., West Bay* ☎ *345/945–5217* ⊕ *www.crackedconch.com.ky.*

Activities

DIVING
SHORE DIVING
Turtle Reef

SCUBA DIVING | The reef begins 20 feet out and gradually descends to a 60-foot miniwall pulsing with sea life and corals of every variety. From there it's just another 15 feet to the dramatic main wall. Ladders provide easy entrance to a shallow cover perfect for predive checks, and because the area isn't buoyed for boats, it's quite pristine. ✉ *West Bay.*

DIVE OPERATORS
★ DiveTech

SCUBA DIVING | **FAMILY** | With comfortable boats and quick access to West Bay, DiveTech offers shore diving at its northwest-coast location, providing loads of interesting creatures, a miniwall, and the North Wall. Technical training (a specialty of owner NJo M Mikutowicz) is unparalleled, and the company offers good, personable service as well as the latest gadgetry such as underwater DPV scooters and rebreathing equipment. They even mix their own gases. Options include extended cross-training Ranger packages, Dive and Art workshop weeks, photography sessions with Tony Land, deep diving, free diving, search and recovery, stingray interaction, reef awareness, and underwater naturalist. Snorkel and diving programs are available for children eight and up, SASY (supplied-air snorkeling, with the unit on a personal flotation device) for five and up. Multiday discounts are a bonus. ✉ *Lighthouse Point , 571 N.W. Point Rd., West Bay* ⊹ *Near Boatswain's Beach* ☎ *345/949–1700, 877/946–5658 Holiday Inn branch* ⊕ *www.divetech.com.*

Indepth Watersports

DIVING/SNORKELING | Indepth Watersports features a state-of-the-art former Navy SEAL RIB (rigid inflatable boat) that enables aficionados to dive both the North Wall and extreme East End on the same trip. They also organize overnights to the Sister Islands. Owner Nat Robb is considered a whiz at technical and rebreathing instruction. Shore dives start at $60; two-tank boat dives start at $125. ✉ *27 Hell Rd., West Bay* ☎ *345/926–8604* ⊕ *www.indepthwatersports.com.*

Sundivers at Cracked Conch Macabuca

SCUBA DIVING | Owned by Ollen Miller, one of Cayman's first dive masters, the on-site dive shop at the Cracked Conch restaurant, next to Boatswain's Beach, offers competitive rates for air, lessons, and rentals; shore access to Turtle Reef; and such amenities as showers, rinse tanks, and storage. They are closed on Tuesday. ⊠ *Cracked Conch, N.W. Point Rd., West Bay* ☎ *345/949–6606.*

FISHING
Bayside Watersports

FISHING | Longtime fisherman Captain Eugene Ebanks established Bayside Watersports in 1974. The family-run West Bay–based company operates two first-class fishing boats, ranging from 31 feet (Lil Hooker) to 53 feet (the *Happy Hooker,* which sleeps six for overnight charters farther afield). The tradition began with the original *Hooker,* named after the Moldcraft Hooker lure and whose team, led by son Al Ebanks, caught a 189.4-pound yellowfin tuna in 1989 that still stands as the island record. They do reef-, tarpon-, and bonefishing trips, but their real specialty is deep-water fishing, such as at 12-Mile Bank, a 3-mile (5-km) strip 90 minutes west of Grand Cayman, where leviathan fighters congregate around the submerged peak of an underwater mountain. ⊠ *Morgan's Harbour, West Bay* ☎ *345/928–2482* ⊕ *www.baysidewatersports.com.*

Captain Asley's Watersports.com

FISHING | This family-run operation prides itself on personable, flexible, and customized charter services for deep-sea, light-tackle, and bonefishing. A privately chartered fishing vessel can run from $750 (small boat, half day) $1,000 (big boat, half-day) to $1,200 (small boat, full day) and $1,600 (big boat, full day). Captain Asley has plied these waters since the 1960s; now his affable, patient kids and extended family (usually Derrin, Dwight, and Kevin) captain the three boats. They're all expert coaches, coaxing a confident approach even from first-timers, though they'll take experts to troll the lesser-known depths; ESPN's Bass Pros selected them as a "preferred outfitter guide." Like many other operators, they also run snorkeling, diving, and sunset and dinner cruises. ☎ *345/949–3054, 345/926–2525* ⊕ *www.caymanfishinguide.com.*

HORSEBACK RIDING
Coral Stone Stables

HORSEBACK RIDING | Leisurely 90-minute horseback rides take in the white-sand beaches at Barkers and inland trails at Savannah; photos are included. Your guide is Noland Stewart, whose ranch contains 20 horses, chickens, and "randy" roosters. Noland offers a nonstop narrative on flora, fauna, and history. He's an

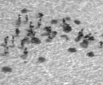

Did You Know?

At popular Stingray Sandbar in Grand Cayman the rays come right up to the excursion boats and will eat out of your hand.

Horseback riding in Barkers National Park

entertaining, endless font of local information, some of it unprintable. Rides are $75; swim rides cost $135. There's a $5 surcharge when paying by credit card. They can also do weddings. ✉ *Conch Point Rd., West Bay* ✛ *Next to Ristorante Pappagallo on left* ☎ *345/916–4799* ⊕ *www.coralstonestables.ky.*

Horseback in Paradise

HORSEBACK RIDING | Gregarious Nicki Eldemire loves telling stories about horse training and life on Cayman. She leads guided tours through Barkers National Park on the West End: an unspoiled peninsular area filled with enthralling plant and animal life along the beaches and wetlands. The steeper price (starting at $90) includes transportation, but it's a private, exclusive experience with no more than four riders per group. And the mounts—mostly Arabians, Paints, and Quarter Horses are magnificent. ✉ *Barkers National Park, Conch Point, West Bay* ☎ *345/945–5839, 345/916–3530* ⊕ *www.caymanhorseriding.com.*

Pampered Ponies

HORSEBACK RIDING | **FAMILY** | Offering "the ultimate tanning machine"—horses walking, trotting, and cantering along the beach—the stable leads private tours and guided trips, including sunset, moonlight, and bareback swim rides along the uninhabited beach from Conch Point to Morgan's Harbour on the north tip beyond West Bay. The charge is US$130 per person for the bareback swim, and US$115 for the basic trek. ✉ *355 Conch Point Rd., West Bay* ☎ *345/945–2262, 345/916–2540* ⊕ *www.ponies.ky.*

Stingray City 👁

Hundreds of gray and khaki Atlantic southern stingrays, resembling inquisitive alien life forms, enact an acrobatic aqua-ballet as they circle this North Sound site seeking handouts from divers and snorkelers. The area actually encompasses two separate locations: Stingray City, called by many the world's greatest 12-foot dive, and the nearby sandbar, where people can wade in waist-deep water.

Steve Irwin's tragic demise rekindled humankind's age-old fear of these beautiful, mysterious "devil" creatures with their barbed tails. The Atlantic southern stingrays are a different, smaller species than the stingray that killed Irwin and as close to tame as possible. Shy and unaggressive by nature, they use their tails only in defense; nonetheless, don't pick rays up unless you follow your guide's careful instructions.

Stingray City's origins can be traced to local fishermen who would moor inside the fringe reef, then clean their catch, tossing the scraps overboard. Captain Marvin Ebanks, who still runs trips in his 90s, recalls feeding them as a child. The rays, who hunt via keen smell (and sensitive electrore-ceptors stippling their under-side, near the mouth), realized they'd discovered their own restaurant and began hanging around. They slowly became inured to human interaction,

rarely displaying the species' typical timidity. They glide like graceful giants (up to 4 feet in diameter), practically nuzzling you with their silken bellies, begging petlike for food. Indeed, crews recognize them (and vice versa), fondly giving the rays nicknames (Hoo-Ray, X-Ray, Gamma Ray), insisting they have distinct personalities.

Instead of teeth, their mouths contain viselike sucking grips. Keep your palms face-up and as flat as possible so they don't unintentionally "swallow" your fingers (their eyes are located atop their bodies, so they hover over and practi-cally hoover your hand in excitement).

More formal visitation guidelines have now been established because 5 to 20 boats visit twice daily, and the population is growing at an alarming rate. Feeding is restricted to appointed tour operators; only natural bait fish like ballyhoo and squid are permitted; the food amount is limited; and any remains and litter must be removed. Many Caymanians and divers oppose altered feeding because it changes the ecosystem's natural food chain. But some concede the good outweighs the bad: the interaction is magical, not to mention fostering greater appreciation and environmen-tal awareness.

SNORKELING

Bayside Watersports, a major fishing outfitter in West Bay, also offers half-day snorkel trips, North Sound beach lunch excursions, Stingray City trips, and dinner cruises. The company operates several popular boats out of West Bay's Morgan Harbour. *See Fishing for more information.*

Ebanks Watersports

SNORKELING | FAMILY | This outfit is run by a large family long known for its aquatic activities. Shawn Ebanks offers a range of water sports, including private charters, scuba diving, fishing, and his popular Sea-Doo wave-runner snorkel tours ($150 for single riders, $200 for two). The crew is friendly, experienced, and particularly adept at holding stingrays for the ultimate photo op; they'll even teach you how to pick one up. Two custom-fitted boats (a 45-foot Garcia and a trim 23-footer) include GPS navigation, VHS radio, freshwater shower, and other necessities. ✉ *164 Yacht Dr., Dock C, West Bay* ☎ *345/925–5273, 345/916–1631, 727/440–5200* ⊕ *www.ebankswatersports.com.*

WINDSURFING

Kitesurf Cayman

WINDSURFING | Here you can take full advantage of the gusty conditions at Barkers Beach. Head instructor Jhon Mora is a member of the Colombian National Kitesurfing Team; lessons, including tricks such as loops and rolls, are geared toward experienced boarders. They also offer hydrofoil lessons ($300 for 1 lesson, or $100/day rental). Group rates are $150 for two hours (private introductory courses are $280); hotel transfers are free with prebooked lessons. ✉ *Barkers, West Bay* ✢ *Near Papagallo's Restaurant* ☎ *345/916–5483* ⊕ *www.kitesurfcayman.com.*

EASTERN DISTRICTS AND NORTH SIDE

Updated by
Monica Walton

👁 Sights   🍴 Restaurants   🛏 Hotels   🛍 Shopping   🍸 Nightlife

★★★★☆   ★★★☆☆   ★★★★☆   ★★★☆☆   ★★★☆☆

NEIGHBORHOOD SPOTLIGHT

TOP EXPERIENCES

- **See the blow holes:** Natural blow holes in the ironshore can be seen on your way to East End.
- **Drink a Rum Point Mudslide:** Made of equal parts Baileys, Kahlua, and Vodka—and it was born at Rum Point.
- **Visit a bioluminiscent bay:** North Side is home to one of the Caribbean's few bioluminescent bays.
- **Relax in Cayman Kai:** Take a dip in the shallow, glasslike waters, snorkel, or shade yourself under a palm tree.
- **Diving:** Known for its more peaceful waters, East End diving is a popular choice for more experienced divers.

GETTING HERE

It's about a 40- to 50-minute drive from Seven Mile Beach to the East End and you can take the leisurely drive or the bus. The buses run Monday through Thursday from 6 am to 11 pm and Friday to Saturday from 6 am to1 am, with limited service on Sunday. Get the 7B bus (with the light-green circle) every 15 minutes from George Town, or the 8A, 9A, or 9B (dark blue, light green, and orange). Free parking is available on-site at all the attractions

PLANNING YOUR TIME

Start your day visiting the blow holes on East End, and then stop off for lunch at Rum Point or Kaibo. Laze all day on the beach or lull yourself to sleep in a hammock in the shade. Visit the warm waters of Starfish Point nearby and stick around until after sunset to experience the magical bioluminescence on a kayak tour around the bay.

QUICK BITES

- **Grape Tree Cafe.** A favorite local spot on the water in the heart of Bodden Town. Try the fried mahimahi with cassava, fritters, honey-glazed plantain, and rice and beans on the side. A great little lunch spot, it's open every day. ⊠ 585 Water Cay Rd., North Side ☎ 345/324–5860 ⊕ www.grapetree-cafe.ky.

- **Kaibo Coffee.** Kaibo is a charming coffeehouse serving gourmet fair-trade coffee and pastries. ⊠ 585 Water Cay Rd., North Side ☎ 345/947–9975 ⊕ www.kaibo.ky/coffee.

- **Over The Edge.** Expertly prepared local fare (Cajun chicken to conch steak to Cayman rock lobster escoveitch) is served with rice and beans, plantains, and fried festival bread at bargain prices, especially at lunch. ⊠ 1148 North Side Rd., Old Man Bay ☎ 345/947–9568.

The eastern districts and north side of Grand Cayman are an easy scenic drive from George Town and Seven Mile Beach (Cayman Kai, on the north side, can even be reached by ferry from George Town). This part of the island is the gateway to hidden crystal coves peppered with starfish, deliciously warm waters, and charming waterfront eateries that ooze character.

Even with picture-perfect views, these more secluded districts remain one of Cayman's best-kept secrets. Although these areas lack the dense commercial development of Seven Mile Beach, they nevertheless house the majority of Grand Cayman residents. Known as the Eastern Districts among locals, Bodden Town, East End, and North Side, which include the south shore of Grand Cayman west of George Town, are the ideal place to stay if you want to avoid crowds.

Bodden Town, the former capital of the Cayman Islands, is on the south shore of the island. It's also the name of the largest district on Grand Cayman, known for its laid-back, easygoing attitude, secluded bays, and quiet streets. Legend has it that the famous pirate Neal Walker made Bodden Town his headquarters and that much treasure is hidden along the coast and in caves. Bodden Town encompasses the residential areas of Savannah and New-lands, where you'll find the 18th-century Mission House. Visitors are also lured by under-the-radar restaurants serving up fried fish and roadside eats. Although Bodden Town is usually only a 20- to 25-minute drive from George Town, make sure you skip rush-hour traffic and venture out on the weekends instead.

About a 40 minute drive from George Town with no traffic, East End is known as the friendly district, packed with deserted beaches and sparkling views of the Caribbean Sea, many will venture out with a picnic or for a quiet stroll along the ironshore. The air is a little breezier out this way, so you might spot kitesurfers skimming along the blue-hued waters; the quiet streets are perfect for cyclists and runners.

Pedro St. James Castle

North Side is home to the tranquil neighborhoods of Cayman Kai and Old Man Bay, where you'll find charming villas peppered along the shoreline. It's about 50 minutes from George Town by car, but accessible by ferry (except Sunday). From hiking the Mastic Trail to exploring the Crystal Caves to tours of the bioluminiscent bay, there's a lot to do despite the quiet. Kaibo Beach Bar and Rum Point both offer casual and fine dining; more local fare is also available at such places as Over the Edge.

Bodden Town

The country's first capital, sleepy Bodden Town, definitely operates on "island time," and the mantra of "soon come" is the way of life. If you're driving, blink and you'll miss it. But the name is also attached to the entire district (the largest on Grand Cayman in terms of area). Stop and relax under one of the colorful cabanas peppered across the buttery-beige shoreline and watch while fishermen happily clean their catch. Charming fish fries are splotched in between sherbert-color Caymanian cottages as well as the national historic site, Mission House.

Sights

Mission House
HISTORIC SITE | This classic gabled two-story Caymanian home on wooden posts, with wattle-and-daub accents, dates to the 1840s

and was restored by the National Trust. The building earned its sobriquet thanks to early missionaries, teachers, and families who lived here while helping establish the Presbyterian ministry and school in Bodden Town. Shards of 19th-century glass and ceramics found on-site and period furnishings are on display. The posted opening hours are irregular, especially during the off-season; tours are by appointment only. ⊠ *63 Gun Square Rd., Bodden Town* ☎ *345/749–1132* ⊕ *www.nationaltrust.org.ky* ▧ *CI$8.*

★ Pedro St. James Castle

HOUSE | Built in 1780, the greathouse is Cayman's oldest stone structure and the island's only remaining late-18th-century residence. In its capacity as courthouse and jail, it was the birthplace of Caymanian democracy, where in December 1831 the first elected parliament was organized and in 1835 the Slavery Abolition Act signed. The structure still has original or historically accurate replicas of sweeping verandas, mahogany floors, rough-hewn wide-beam ceilings, outside louvers, stone and oxblood- or mustard-color limewashed walls, brass fixtures, and Georgian furnishings (from tea caddies to canopy beds to commodes). Paying obsessive attention to detail, the curators even fill glasses with faux wine. The minimuseum also includes a hodgepodge of displays from slave emancipation to old stamps. The buildings are surrounded by 8 acres of natural parks and woodlands. You can stroll through landscaping of native Caymanian flora and experience one of the most spectacular views on the island from atop the dramatic Great Pedro Bluff. First watch the impressive multimedia show, on the hour, complete with smoking pots, misting rains, and two screens. The poignant Hurricane Ivan Memorial outside uses text, images, and symbols to represent important aspects of the 2004 disaster. A branch of Cayman Spirits brings history further to life with rum tastings. ⊠ *305 Pedro Castle Rd., Savannah, Bodden Town* ☎ *345/947–3329* ⊕ *www.pedrostjames. ky* ▧ *CI$10.*

Restaurants

Czech Inn Bar and Grill

$ | **CARIBBEAN** | A popular roadside grill offering Czech foods, steaks, and jerk chicken from chef Jiri Zitterbart is tucked away in Pease Bay, Bodden Town. This ramshackle bar has grown somewhat of a devoted following in a short time. **Known for:** classic Caymanian dishes; terrific takeout; great lobster. ⑤ *Average main: $10* ⊠ *563 Bodden Town Rd., Bodden Town* ☎ *345/939–3474.*

Rum Point

Rum Point

Water Cay

Starfish Point

Water Cay

Cayman Kai

Drift Wood Village

North Side Road

North Side

Brinkleys

Hutland

Malportas Pond

Further Ground

Booby Cay

North Sound Estates

Midland Acres

Breakers

Northward

Belford Estates

Pease Bay

Bodden Town Rd.

North Cayman Palms

Pease Bay

Savannah

South Cayman Palms

Bodden Town

Bodden Bay

0	1 mi
0	1 km

LITTLE CAYMAN

CAYMAN BRAC

GRAND CAYMAN

KEY	
❶	*Exploring Sights*
❶	*Restaurants*
❶	*Hotels*

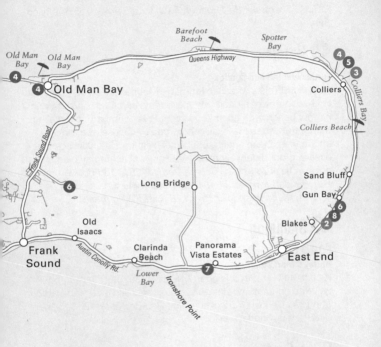

Eastern Districts and North Side

Caribbean Sea

Barefoot Beach
Spotter Bay
Old Man Bay
Old Man Bay
Queens Highway
4
5
3
Old Man Bay
4
Colliers
Colliers Bay
4
Frank Sound Road
Colliers Beach
Sand Bluff
Long Bridge
Gun Bay
6
6
8 **2**
Blakes
Old Isaacs
Clarinda Beach
Panorama Vista Estates
East End
Frank Sound
Austin Conolly Rd.
Lower Bay
7
Ironshore Point

Sights

Bioluminiscent Bay, **3**

Blowholes, **7**

Crystal Caves, **4**

Mastic Trail, **5**

Mission House, **2**

Pedro St. James Castle, **1**

Queen Elizabeth II Botanic Park, **6**

Wreck of the Ten Sails Park, **8**

Restaurants

Czech Inn Bar and Grill, **3**

Kaibo Beach Bar and Grill, **1**

Over the Edge, **4**

Rankin's Jerk Centre, **2**

Tides, **5**

Vivine's Kitchen, **6**

Hotels

Compass Point Dive Resort, **2**

Morritt's Tortuga Club and Resort, **3**

Turtle Nest Inn and Condos, **1**

Wyndham Reef Resort Grand Cayman, **4**

Rankin's Jerk Centre

$$ | CARIBBEAN | A faux cow and pig greet you, and you can savor Miss Rankin's scrumptious turtle stew, lobster curry, and jerk dishes in her alluring garden. Don't miss her homemade bread pudding for dessert. **Known for:** pretty garden seating; traditional Caymanian fare; great place to meet locals. ⑤ *Average main: $12* ✉ *3032 Shamrock Rd., Bodden Town* ☎ *345/947–3155* ⊗ *Closed Sun.*

Hotels

Turtle Nest Inn and Condos

$ | RENTAL | This affordable, intimate, Mediterranean-style seaside inn has roomy one-bedroom apartments and a pool overlooking a narrow beach with good snorkeling. **Pros:** wonderful snorkeling; thoughtful extras like a car rental, free Wi-Fi, use of a mobile phone, and cheap equipment rentals; caring staff. **Cons:** car necessary; ground-floor room views slightly obscured by palms; road noise in back rooms. ⑤ *Rooms from: $199* ✉ *166 Bodden Town Rd., Bodden Town* ☎ *345/947–8665* ⊕ *www.turtlenestinn.com, www.turtlenestcondos.com* ⇌ *18 units* ⑪ *No meals.*

Shopping

FOOD

Hurley's Marketplace

FOOD/CANDY | Hurley's is open Monday–Saturday 7 am–11 pm. It's well-known for its hot take-out dinner specials. ✉ *Grand Harbour Shopping Centre, 1053 Crewe Rd., Red Bay Estate* ☎ *345/947–8488* ⊕ *www.hurleys.ky.*

East End

Fancy a leg-pumping hike surrounded by inspiring nature or an afternoon flopped out on deliciously warm sands? East End has you covered. The home of the Mastic Trail, this district is rammed full of stunning scenery and a view of the Caribbean sea that melts from one shade of blue to the next. Quintessentially Caribbean and delightfully charming, a trip to East End is worth the drive.

The Lowdown on Rundown

Rundown is a steamy Caymanian fish stew combining a potpourri of ingredients. A rundown is also a quick summary, and this enduringly popular show performed annually in October since 1991 puns on both definitions. The format is a series of skits, music, stand-up comedy, monologues, cabaret, dance, and impersonations—written from scratch each year by playwright-actor Dave Martins: a light-hearted, topical, satirical lampoon of daily Caymanian life, current events, politics, personalities, and nationalities. Caymanians call it their answer to *The Daily Show* and *Colbert Report*.

Martins started Rundown because he'd "seen topical shows in other Caribbean countries ... and felt something similar would work here, but Cayman is very conservative and people said that would get me in hot water." After seeing caricatures of prominent people hanging in their offices, "I concluded that Caymanians were ready to laugh at themselves and wrote the first show. Some of the cast were very apprehensive in rehearsals, but it was a hit from day one." Every year provides fodder and inspiration

aplenty, but the show is more gently mocking than controversial, and the targets of its barbs usually laugh along with everyone else.

The audience's nonstop guffawing may bemuse tourists. Martins explains, "A lot of the stuff I write ... is very contextual and almost always local, so the lyrics generally make little sense to someone outside that frame." Recent skits spoofed the red tape involved in putting up a little backyard shed to play dominoes; interplay among a crowd of people lining up to get Caymanian Immigration Status (the rollover policy); a Jamaican trying to teach a Londoner to speak the J dialect; and a lost tourist trying to get directions from a group that includes a Cuban, a Barbadian, a Pakistani, a Jamaican, a Chinaman, and, of course, a Caymanian ... " all of whom are incomprehensible to the visitor. ... To understand it fully, you'd need to have lived here 10, 15 years." He doesn't Americanize or clean up the dialect, but that augments the honest authenticity. And much of the material, from frustrating daily interactions to bureaucratic blundering, transcends any cultural divide.

◉ Sights

Blowholes

NATURE SITE | FAMILY | When the easterly trade winds blow hard, crashing waves force water into caverns and send impressive geysers shooting up as much as 20 feet through the ironshore. The blowholes were partially filled during Hurricane Ivan in 2004, so the water must be rough to recapture their former elemental drama. ☒ *Frank Sound Rd., roughly 10 miles (16 km) east of Bodden Town, near East End.*

Mastic Trail

TRAIL | This significant trail, used in the 1800s as the only direct path to the North Side, is a rugged 2-mile (3-km) slash through 776 dense acres of woodlands, black mangrove swamps, savanna, agricultural remnants, and ancient rock formations. It encompasses more than 700 species of flora and fauna, including Cayman's largest remaining contiguous ancient forest of mastic trees (one of the heavily deforested Caribbean's last examples). A comfortable walk depends on weather—winter is better because it's drier, though flowering plants such as the banana orchid blaze in summer. Call the National Trust to determine suitability and to book a guide ($30); tours run Tuesday through Friday morning by appointment. Or walk on the wild side with a $5 guidebook covering the ecosystems, endemic wildlife, seasonal changes, poisonous plants, and folkloric uses of flora. The trip takes about three hours. ☒ *Frank Sound Rd., East End* ✠ *Entrance by fire station at botanic park, Breakers* ☎ *345/749–1121, 345/749–1124 for guide reservations* ⊕ *www.nationaltrust.org.ky.*

Wreck of the Ten Sails Park

CITY PARK | This lonely, lovely park on Grand Cayman's windswept eastern tip commemorates the island's most (in)famous shipwreck. On February 8, 1794, the *Cordelia,* heading a convoy of 58 square-rigged merchant vessels en route from Jamaica to England, foundered on one of the treacherous East End reefs. Its warning cannon fire was tragically misconstrued as a call to band more closely together due to imminent pirate attack, and nine more ships ran aground. Local sailors, who knew the rough seas, demonstrated great bravery in rescuing all 400-odd seamen. Popular legend claims (romantically but inaccurately) that King George III granted the islands an eternal tax exemption. Queen Elizabeth II dedicated the park's plaque in 1994. Interpretive signs document the historic details. The ironically peaceful headland provides magnificent views of the reef (including more recent shipwrecks); bird-watching is superb from here half a mile south along the coast to the Lighthouse Park, perched on a craggy bluff. ⊠ *Austin Conolly Dr., East End* ☎ *345/949–0121 National Trust* 🖾 *Free.*

Beaches

Barefoot Beach

BEACH—SIGHT | Famous for its postcard-perfect views, Barefoot beach is one of the East End's best beaches, offering soft white sand, crystal clear shallow waters, and a shady cabana. It's a favorite spot for locals and tourists, who come on Sunday to watch the fishing boats out at sea. **Amenities:** parking (free). **Best for:** solitude; snorkeling; walking. ⊠ *East End.*

Colliers Beach

BEACH—SIGHT | Just drive along and look for any sandy beach, park your car, and enjoy a stroll. The vanilla-hue stretch at Colliers Bay, by the Reef and Morritt's resorts (which offer water sports), is a good, clean one with superior snorkeling. **Amenities:** food and drink; water sports. **Best for:** snorkeling; solitude; sunrise; walking. ⊠ *Queen's Hwy., Colliers, East End.*

 Restaurants

Tides

$$$$ | **ECLECTIC** | The Wyndham Reef Resort's all-purpose dining room (formerly known as Pelican's Reef) converts into a refined space come evening, its marine murals and nautical paraphernalia (rigging, fish nets) illuminated by candles, with clever partitioning by framed sails to enhance its intimacy. Most of the kitchen hails from the Caribbean, but even the buffets merrily marry culinary influences from India to Italy; they'll infuse hummus with saffron and spike spring rolls with wasabi. **Known for:** Barefoot Man performances; bountiful buffets; marine decor. ⑤ *Average main: $40* ⊠ *Wyndham Reef Resort Grand Cayman, 2221 Queen's Hwy., Colliers* ☎ *345/947–3100, 345/516–0218* ⊕ *www.wyndhamcayman.com* ☉ *No lunch.*

Vivine's Kitchen

$$ | **CARIBBEAN** | Cars practically block the road at this unprepossessing hot spot for classic Caymanian food—literally Vivine and Ray Watler's home. Prime seating is in the waterfront courtyard, serenaded by rustling seagrape leaves, crashing surf, and screeching gulls. **Known for:** authentic Caymanian food; typical island hospitality; good prices for giant portions. ⑤ *Average main: $17* ⊠ *Austin Dr., Gun Bay, East End* ☎ *345/947–7435* ▭ *No credit cards.*

Getting SASY 🏃

A few years ago, Wayne Hasson, a Cayman resident and owner of the live-aboard dive boat *Cayman Aggressor*, faced a dilemma. He and his wife, Anne, were both ardent, accomplished scuba divers and marine environmentalists. His children, then five and seven, understandably longed to share the diving experience, but their mother insisted that they simply snorkel atop the surface until they reached the age minimum of 12. They hated breathing in water and sputtering. So Hasson developed an ingenious compromise device that has already profoundly impacted the scuba industry and ocean education.

Hasson rigged a life vest with a pony bottle and regulator and let his kids try breathing from an air tank while positively buoyant at the surface. They remained face down without inhaling water, mimicking the feel of actual diving. The family worked on R&D for nearly a year with Custom Buoyancy, inventing and refining SASY (Supplied Air Snorkeling for Youth). The units resemble the real thing with life vest, small scuba tank (13 cubic feet as opposed

to 19) in an adjustable holder, and regulator (all integrating crucial safety features like child-proof attachments and stabilizing straps); any kid five or older could now enjoy "diving" with Mom and Dad safely and comfortably. Recognizing adults might also feel awkward with snorkeling gear, Hasson created SASA (Supplied Air Snorkeling for Adults), which differs in the tank size (19 to 30 cubic feet). Although "snuba" allows you to go underwater, the hose can prove cumbersome and restrict the scope of your movement; kids as young as four can enjoy the feel of dive equipment with SASY, but the snuba minimum age is eight.

The device promotes interest in diving from a younger age, but equally important, the patent, trademarks, and income from sales and licensing agreements belong to Oceans for Youth, a nonprofit organization the Hassons subsequently founded to educate youth about the marine environment and the vital connection between sea and land life. As Hasson states, " ... the health of the world's oceans will soon become the responsibility of today's children."

Eating at a Home Kitchen

Aspiring Anthony Bourdains on Grand Cayman should seek out roadside vans, huts, kiosks, and stalls dishing out unfamiliar grub. These casual spots offer authentic fare at very fair prices, with main dishes and heaping helpings of sides costing under CI\$10. If you thought Mickey D's special sauce or Coke was a secret formula, try prying prized recipes handed down for generations from these islanders.

Captain Herman's Fish Fry. You can't miss the vibrant marine life mural and key lime-color walls topped by a roof adorned with conch shells at this seaside spot beloved for sweet-and-sour shrimp, oxtail and beans, conch chowder, and more. ☒ *Sea View Rd. off Indiana La., East End, Grand Cayman* ☏ 345/924–4007.

Czech Inn Bar and Grill. The Czech Inn has developed a following for its Czech food and jerk chicken. ☒ *563 Bodden Town Rd., Bodden Town, Grand Cayman* ☏ 345/939–3474.

Rankin's Jerk Centre. A faux cow and pig greet you at Rankin's Jerk Centre, where you can savor Miss Rankin's scrumptious turtle stew and jerk dishes in her alluring garden. ☒ *3032 Shamrock Rd., Bodden Town, Grand Cayman* ☏ 345/947–3155.

Two of these most casual eateries on the island are George Town institutions.

Heritage Kitchen. West Bay's popular family-run Heritage Kitchen serves up legendary raconteur Tunny Powell's fish tea, barbecue ribs, and fish fry—with a generous portion of local lore. It's only open sporadically, so look for it when you're in the area. ☒ *Just off Boggy Sand Rd., West Bay, Grand Cayman.*

Tony's Jerk Foods. Even politicos stand in line at Tony's Jerk Foods, which serves everything from cow foot to conch stew (you can't miss the exterior's beach mural). ☒ *193 School Rd., George Town, Grand Cayman* ☏ 345/916–6860.

Hotels

Compass Point Dive Resort

$$ | RESORT | This tranquil, congenial getaway run by the admirable Ocean Frontiers scuba operation would steer even nondivers in the right direction, from the powder-blue buildings elevated on stilts with white columns and trim to the interiors' contrasting granite accents and sparkling white-tile floors with luscious lemon, tomato, and peach walls and vivid marine photos. **Pros:** top-notch dive operation; free bike/kayak use; good value, especially

Cayman House and Garden

The few original Caymanian cottages that exist represent a unique architectural vernacular cannily adapted to the climate and available resources. Foundation posts and floors were constructed from durable, termite-resistant ironwood. Wattle-and-daub walls were fashioned from basket-woven sticks plastered on both sides with lime daub (extracted coral burned with various woods). The earliest roofs were thatched with woven palm fronds (later shingled or topped with corrugated zinc); their peaks helped cool houses, as hot air rises. The kitchen was separate, usually just a "caboose" stove for cooking.

The other unusual custom, "backing sand," originated as a Christmas tradition, then became a year-round decorative statement. Women and children would tote woven-thatch baskets by moonlight to the beach, bringing "back" glittering white sand to cover their front yards. They'd rake intricate patterns and adorn the sand with sinuous conch-shell paths. The yard was also swept Saturday so it would look well tended after Sunday services. A side benefit was that it helped reduce insect infestation.

packages. **Cons:** isolated location requires a car; conservation is admirable but air-conditioning can't go too low; poky beaches with poor swim access. ⑤ *Rooms from: $299* ✉ *346 Austin Conolly Dr., Gun Bay, East End* ☎ *345/947–7500, 800/348–6096, 345/947–0000* ⊕ *www.compasspointdiveresort.com* ⌁ *29 condos* ⦿ *No meals.*

Morritt's Tortuga Club and Resort

$$ | **RESORT** | Morritt's Tortuga Club and Resort offers 146 well-maintained, fully equipped, mostly timeshare units, albeit many lacking beach views and/or access (the best and priciest are branded "The Londoner" and "Grand Resort"). **Pros:** excellent day spa; Tortuga Divers and Red Sail Sports on site; great snorkeling. **Cons:** many units lack beach views and access; many units are dated; not for those who want to be in the center of the action. ⑤ *Rooms from: $279* ✉ *1 Queens Hwy., East End* ☎ *345/947–7449, 877/667–7488* ⊕ *www.morritts.com* ⌁ *146 rooms* ⦿ *No meals.*

Wyndham Reef Resort Grand Cayman

$$ | **RESORT** | **FAMILY** | Casual elegance prevails throughout this exceedingly well-run time-share property, which straddles a 600-foot beach on the less hectic East End. Each villa has a roomy terrace facing the sea; two-bedroom units can be partitioned, but even the studio has Wi-Fi, a DVD player, microwave, and fridge. **Pros:** romantically remote; AI packages and online discounts available; enthusiastic staff (including a crackerjack wedding coordinator). **Cons:** remote; few dining options nearby; glorious beach but often a seaweed problem. $ *Rooms from: $349* ✉ *2221 Queen's Hwy., Colliers, East End* ☎ *345/947–3100, 888/232–0541* ⊕ *www. wyndhamcayman.com* ⇨ *152 suites* ⦿ *No meals.*

Nightlife

BARS
The Beach Bar
BARS/PUBS | This spot draws an eclectic group of dive masters, expats, honeymooners, and mingling singles. The knockout, colorful cocktails pack quite a punch, making the sunset last for hours. The bar dialogue is entertainment enough, but don't miss local legend, country-calypsonian Barefoot Man, when he plays "upstairs" at Tides—he's to Cayman what Jimmy Buffett is to Key West. ✉ *Wyndham Reef Resort Grand Cayman, 2221 Queen's Hwy., Colliers, East End* ☎ *345/947–3100* ⊕ *www.wyndhamcayman.com.*

★ South Coast Bar and Grill
BARS/PUBS | This delightful seaside slice of old Cayman—grizzled regulars slamming down dominoes, fabulous sea views, old model cars, Friday-night dances to local legend Lammie, karaoke Saturday with Elvis impersonator Errol Dunbar, and reasonably priced red conch chowder and jerk chicken sausage—is also a big politico hangout. Fascinating photos, some historical, show local scenes and personalities. The juke jives, from Creedence Clearwater Revival to Mighty Sparrow. ✉ *2035 Bodden Town Rd., Breakers, East End* ☎ *345/947–2517* ⊕ *www.southcoastbar.com.*

Activities

BIKING
Eco Rides Cayman
BICYCLING | Green excursions that don't cost too many greenbacks are the house specialty, winding through the serene East End. The five routes ($70–$100) run from a scenic coastal route hugging the littoral without stopping, to a "cave trek" and "inland escape" that showcases natural topography—caverns, blowholes, and local farms. Hybrid rentals ($40/day) are available upon request. ✉ *2708 Seaview Dr., East End* ☎ *345/922–0754* ⊕ *www.ecoridescayman.ky.*

Blue Dragons

Cosponsored by the Botanic Park and the National Trust, the **Blue Iguana Recovery Program** (⊕ www.blueiguana. ky) is a model captive breeding plan for the remarkable reptiles that only two decades ago faced total extinction. The Grand Cayman blue iguana lived on the island for millennia until man arrived, its only natural predator the racer snake. Until recently they were the world's most critically endangered species, functionally extinct with only 25 remaining in the wild. BIRP has released more than 300 into the Salina Reserve, with an ultimate repopulation goal of 1,000 if they can breed successfully in the wild.

The National Trust conducts safaris six mornings a week, giving you a chance to see hatchlings in the cages, camouflaged toddlers, and breeding-age adults like Mad Max and Blue Blue. Most of the iguanas raised here are released at two years by the Wildlife Conservation Society with a microchip implant tag for radio tracking and color-coded beading for unique identification. Tones fluctuate according to lighting and season, brightening to azure during the April–May breeding period. Guides explain the gestation and incubation periods and the pairing of potential mates. Sadly, you'll also learn why the breeding program is on temporary hiatus: a mysterious bacterium affecting the blues.

If you can't make it to the park, look for the 15 larger-than-life, one-of-a-kind outdoor sculptures commissioned from local artists scattered around the island. You can download maps of the Blue Dragon Trail from the BIRP, National Trust, and Botanic Park sites. Many hotels also stock leaflets with maps and fun facts (the iguanas live up to 70 years, grow to 6 feet in length, and weigh 25 pounds). You can even purchase custom blue iguana products (helping fund research), such as Joel Friesch's limited-edition hand-painted bobbleheads (blues bob their heads rapidly as a territorial warning) packaged in a bright-yellow, hard cardboard box. You can also volunteer for a working vacation (or longer fieldwork study stint) online.

BIRD-WATCHING
Silver Thatch Tours
BIRD WATCHING | Geddes Hislop, who knows his birds and his island (though he's Trinidadian by birth), runs customizable five-hour natural and historic heritage tours ($50 an hour up to four people), including the Queen Elizabeth II Botanic Park's nature trail and lake and other prime birding spots. Serious birders leave at dawn. Prearranged tours include a guide, pickup and return transport, and refreshments—a great excuse to discuss herbal medicinal folklore. ☎ *345/925–7401* ⊕ *birdingpal.org/Cayman.htm.*

DIVING
DIVE OPERATORS
★ Ocean Frontiers
SCUBA DIVING | This excellent ecocentric operation offers friendly small-group diving and a technical training facility, exploring the less trammeled, trafficked East End. The company provides valet service, personalized attention, a complimentary courtesy shuttle, and an emphasis on green initiatives and specialized diving, including unguided computer, technical, nitrox instructor, underwater naturalist, and cave diving for advanced participants. You can even participate in lionfish culls. There's a wonderful Skills Review and Tune-Up course so beginners or rusty divers won't feel over their heads. Special touches include hot chocolate and homemade muffins on night dives; the owner, Steve, will arrange for a minister to conduct weddings in full face masks. ✉ *Compass Point, 346 Austin Connelly Dr., East End* ☎ *345/640–7500, 800/348–6096 toll-free, 345/947–0000, 954/727–5312 Vonage toll-free in U.S.* ⊕ *www.oceanfrontiers.com.*

WINDSURFING
Cayman Windsurfing with Red Sail Sports at Morritt's
WINDSURFING | This company offers a full range of top-flight equipment as well as lessons. Rentals on top-of-the-line, regularly updated equipment start at $40 per hour. ✉ *Morritt's Tortuga Resort, Colliers, East End* ☎ *345/947–2097* ⊕ *www.tortugadivers. com.*

North Side

North Side is the district farthest away from Seven Mile Beach and George Town, where most tourists tend to go, and tucked at the top of the island, but it has the lot: majestic caves hundreds of thousands of years old; Instagram-worthy shorelines glimmering in the sunlight; and authentic Caribbean eateries that make you

The Crystal Caves are part of a large system of caverns in the limestone underneath Grand Cayman.

feel like you belong. Strap yourself in: North Side is worth going further for.

Cayman's best kept secret, Cayman Kai, is a quaint community near Rum Point, where tranquillity and nature are in abundance. Home to Grand Cayman's magical bioluminescent bay, Cayman Kai is also the birthplace of the award-winning milk shake known as the "Mudslide," a must-try when you're in town. Made of equal parts Molly's or Baileys Irish Cream, Kahlua, and Vodka, a dusting of cinnamon, and a Maraschino cherry on top, it's more boozy than it tastes, so watch your step. Kaibo & Rum Point Wreck Bar both have their own take on the famed recipe, as well as just-off-the-boat mahimahi and grilled-to-perfection pizzas. For something more local, try the conch fritters. While you're there, take a dip in the shallow, glasslike waters, and snorkel or shade yourself under a palm tree.

Sights

★ Bioluminiscent Bay

BODY OF WATER | Grand Cayman's bioluminiscent bay, near Rum Point, is one of the few such bays in the world. It's about 45 minutes from George Town and can be visited on a guided tour. The bioluminscent dinoflaggelates are visible for a couple of weeks every month, but not at all times. The local tour operators know the best times to visit and schedule tours for those nights (especially when there is no full moon). ⊠ *Rum Point.*

★ Crystal Caves

CAVE | **FAMILY** | At the end of a seemingly endless, bumpy road, your guide takes you on a short hike to the "treehouse" refreshment-souvenir stand of this Grand Cayman locale. A viewing platform provides breathtaking vistas of a ginormous banyan tree framing the first cave entrance. Currently, three large caverns in the extensive network have been opened and outfitted with wood pathways and strategic lighting. Millions of years ago, the network was submerged underwater (a subterranean lake serves as a hauntingly lovely reminder); the land gradually rose over millennia. Nature has fashioned extraordinary crystal gardens and "fish-scale" columns from delicate, fragile flowstone; part of the fun is identifying the fanciful shapes whimsically carved by the stalactites and stalagmites. The 90-minute tours are offered on the hour from 9 am through 4 pm. Ambitious plans include adding ziplines and 4WD trails. If you're going on to tour the East End, look for the fascinating little Davidoff's sculpture garden (depicting local critters) along the coastal highway just outside the caves. ⊠ 69 Northside Rd., Old Man Bay, North Side ☎ 345/949–2283, 345/925–3001 ⊕ www.caymancrystalcaves.com ☒ $40.

★ Queen Elizabeth II Botanic Park

NATURE PRESERVE | **FAMILY** | This 65-acre wilderness preserve showcases a wide range of indigenous and nonindigenous tropical vegetation, approximately 2,000 species in total. Splendid sections include numerous water features from limpid lily ponds to cascades; a Heritage Garden with a traditional cottage and "caboose" (outside kitchen) that includes crops that might have been planted on Cayman a century ago; and a Floral Colour Garden arranged by color, the walkway wandering through sections of pink, red, orange, yellow, white, blue, mauve, lavender, and purple. A 2-acre lake and adjacent wetlands include three islets that provide a habitat and breeding ground for native birds just as showy as the floral displays: green herons, black-necked stilts, American coots, blue winged teal, cattle egrets, and rare West Indian whistling ducks. The nearly mile-long Woodland Trail encompasses every Cayman ecosystem from wetland to cactus thicket, buttonwood swamp to lofty woodland with imposing mahogany trees. You'll encounter birds, lizards, turtles, and agoutis, but the park's star residents are the protected endemic blue iguanas, found only in Grand Cayman. The world's most endangered iguana, they're the focus of the National Trust's Blue Iguana Recovery Program, a captive breeding and reintroduction facility. This section of the park is usually closed to the public, though released "blue dragons" hang out in the vicinity. The Trust conducts 90-minute behind-the-scenes safaris

Queen Elizabeth II Botanic Park is filled with local flora and fauna, including the endangered Cayman blue iguana.

Monday through Saturday at 11 am for $30. ⊠ *367 Botanic Rd., North Side* ☎ *345/947–9462* ⊕ *www.botanic-park.ky* ⊠ *CI$10.*

Beaches

Old Man Bay

BEACH—SIGHT | The North Side features plenty of hidden coves and pristine stretches of perfect sand, where you'll be disturbed only by seabirds dive-bombing for lunch and the occasional lone fishers casting nets for sprats, then dumping them into buckets. Over the Edge restaurant is less than 1 mile (1½ km) west. Otherwise, it's fairly undeveloped for miles, save for the occasional private home. Snorkeling is spectacular when waters are calm. **Amenities:** food and drink. **Best for:** snorkeling; solitude; walking. ⊠ *Queen's Hwy., Old Man Bay, North Side* ✛ *Just off Frank Sound Rd.*

Rum Point Beach

BEACH—SIGHT | This North Sound beach has hammocks slung in towering casuarina trees, picnic tables, casual and "fancier" dining options, a well-stocked shop for seaworthy sundries, and Red Sail Sports, which offers various water sports and boats to explore Stingray City. The barrier reef ensures safe snorkeling and soft sand. The bottom remains shallow for a long way from shore, but it's littered with small coral heads, so be careful. The Wreck is an ultracasual hangout serving outstanding pub grub from fish-and-chips to wings, as well as lethal Mudslide cocktails.

Just around the bend, another quintessential beach hangout, Kaibo, rocks during the day. **Amenities:** food and drink; parking (no fee); showers; toilets; water sports. **Best for:** partiers; snorkeling. ⊠ *Rum Point, North Side.*

Starfish Point

BEACH—SIGHT | A remote beach just off the northern coast of Cayman, Starfish Point attracts beautiful starfish to its turtle grass–lined shores and emerald green, warm waters. Watch the sunset, wade in the water and explore the sandy shoreline. **Amenities:** parking (free). **Best for:** solitude; sunset; walking. ⊠ *Rum Point, North Side.*

Water Cay

BEACH—SIGHT | If you want an isolated, unspoiled beach, bear left at Rum Point, on the North Side, and follow the road to the end. When you pass a porte cochere for an abandoned condo development, you'll see the soft, sandy beach. Wade out knee deep and look for the large, flame-hue starfish. (Don't touch—just look.) Locals also call it Starfish or Ivory Point. **Amenities:** none. **Best for:** solitude; swimming. ⊠ *North Side.*

🍴 Restaurants

Kaibo Beach Bar and Grill

$$$ | **CARIBBEAN** | Overlooking the North Sound, this beach hangout rocks days (fantastic lunches that cost half the price of dinner, festive atmosphere including impromptu volleyball tourneys, and free Wi-Fi) and serves murderous margaritas and mudslides well into the evening to boisterous yachties, locals, sports buffs, and expats. Enjoy smoked mahimahi pâté, brick-oven pizzas, hefty burgers, and wondrous wraps, either on the multitier seafood platter and Christmas lights or in hammocks and thatched cabanas amid the palms. **Known for:** boisterous crowd; fun beach events; top-notch pub grub. ⑤ *Average main: $21* ⊠ *585 Water Cay Rd., Rum Point, North Side* ☎ *345/947–9975* ⊕ *www.kaibo.ky.*

Over the Edge

$$$ | **CARIBBEAN** | This fun, funky seaside spot brims with character and characters (a soused regular might welcome you by reciting "the daily lunch special: chilled barley soup … That's beer"). **Known for:** delectable local fare; island insiders' hangout; appealing semi-enclosed patio. ⑤ *Average main: $24* ⊠ *312 North Side Rd., Old Man Bay, North Side* ☎ *345/947–9568.*

Activities

KAYAKING
★ Cayman Kayaks

KAYAKING | FAMILY | Even beginners find the tours easy (the guides dub it low-impact aerobics), and the sit-on-top tandem kayaks are stable and comfortable. The Bio Bay tour involves more strenuous paddling, but the underwater light show is magical as millions of bioluminescent microorganisms called dinoflagellates glow like fireflies when disturbed. It runs only on moonless nights and books well in advance. Passionate environmentalists, owners Tom and Lisha Watling, devised a way to limit exposure of harmful repellent and sunscreen: they designed a "black box" electric boat with a viewing hole at the bottom, as well as high walls that focus your glimpse of the stars above. Tours ($59–$69 with some kids' and group discounts) depart from different locations, most from the public access jetty to the left of Rum Point. They've temporarily discontinued the mangrove wetlands tour, but it's a splendid learning experience when it runs, providing an absorbing discussion of indigenous animals (including a mesmerizing stop at a gently pulsing, nonstinging Cassiopeia jellyfish pond) and plants, the effects of hurricanes, and conservation efforts. ⊠ *Rum Point Club, North Side, Rum Point* ☎ *345/746–3249, 345/926–4467* ⊕ *www.caymankayaks.com.*

SNORKELING
Red Sail Sports

SNORKELING | FAMILY | Luxurious 62- and 65-foot catamarans (the *Spirits of Cayman, Poseidon, Calypso,* and *Ppalu)* often carry large groups on Stingray City, sunset, and evening sails ($45–$90, $25–$45 children under 12) including dinner in winter. Although the service may not be personal, it's efficient. A glass-bottom boat takes passengers to Stingray City/Sandbar and nearby coral reefs. Trips run from several hotels, including the Westin and Morritt's, in addition to the Rum Point headquarters. ⊠ *Rum Point, North Side* ☎ *345/949–8745, 345/623–5965, 877/506–6368* ⊕ *www. redsailcayman.com.*

CAYMAN BRAC

Updated by
Monica Walton

⊙ **Sights** 🍴 **Restaurants** 🛏 **Hotels** 🛍 **Shopping** 🍸 **Nightlife**
★★★★★   ★★★★★   ★★★★★   ★★★★★   ★★★★★

WELCOME TO CAYMAN BRAC

TOP REASONS TO GO

★ **Diving.** From walls and wrecks to underwater installations, this is a great dive destination.

★ **Lighthouse walk.** Offering thrilling Caribbean vistas and a look at nature's fierce elemental savagery.

★ **Local crafts.** Several "old timer" artisans keep traditions alive.

★ **Caving.** Several caves are accessible—and have played a vital role in sheltering islanders during storms.

★ **Museum-hop.** The Cayman Brac Museum pays tribute to this remote island's maritime tradition.

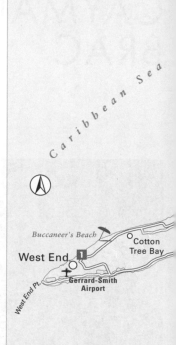

1 **West End.** In Cayman Brac's West End you will find the airport, two grocery stores, a gas station, and a few condo complexes. The West End has the highest population of residents on the island as well as the infamous wreck dive, M.V. *Capt. Keith Tibbetts* just offshore.

2 **Stake Bay.** On the north side, the island's capital lies in the middle of the island. It's a small town that is home to the single

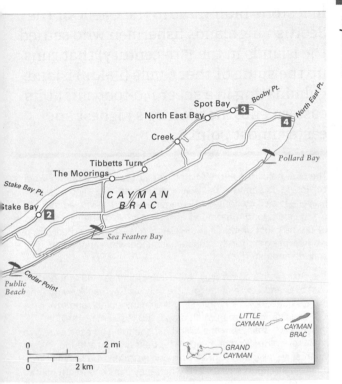

Spot Bay
North East Bay
Booby Pt.
Creek
North East Pt.
Pollard Bay
Tibbetts Turn
The Moorings
Stake Bay Pt.
CAYMAN BRAC
Stake Bay
Sea Feather Bay
Cedar Point
Public Beach

0 _____ 2 mi
0 _____ 2 km

LITTLE CAYMAN
CAYMAN BRAC
GRAND CAYMAN

government building, the hospital, the museum, a grocery store, and the island's only high school.

3 Spot Bay. Continue east to Watering Place, Creek, and Spot Bay. On the north shore near East End, you'll find quaint little stores and restaurants offering authentic souvenirs and traditional Caymanian eats in Watering Place, Creek, and Spot Bay. The pretty and charming Cayman Brac Heritage House is also located between Creek and Spot Bay.

4 East End. The island's East End will eventually lead you to the limestone cliffs, including the notorious 140-foot Bluff, offering panoramic views of the Caribbean Sea.

Cayman Brac is named for its most distinctive feature—a moody, craggy limestone bluff (*brac* in the Gaelic of the Scottish highlands fishermen who settled the islands in the 18th century) that runs up the spine of the 12-mile (19-km) island, culminating in a sheer 140-foot cliff at its eastern end, the country's highest and easternmost point.

The bluff holds the angry Atlantic at bay, gradually tapering like a coil losing its spring in the west. Nature's artistry—and awesome power—is also evident in the many caves and sinkholes that stipple the crag, long rumored to hold pirates' gold. The islandscape is by far the most dramatic in the Cayman Islands, though divers the world over come for the spectacular underwater topography and sponge-encrusted wrecks.

The Brac, as it's commonly called, sits 90 miles (143 km) northeast of Grand Cayman, accessible only via Cayman Airways (and private boat), but it's nothing like the cosmopolitan and Americanized Grand Cayman. With only 2,100 residents—they call themselves Brackers—the island has the feel and easy pace of a small town. Brackers are known for their friendly attitude toward visitors, so it's easy to strike up a conversation. You're never treated like a stranger; locals wave when they pass and might invite you home for a traditional rundown (a thick, sultry fish stew) and storytelling, usually about the sea, the turtle schooners, and the great hurricane of 1932 (when the caves offered shelter to islanders). Brackers are as calm and peaceful as their island is rugged, having been violently sculpted by sea and wind, most recently by Hurricane Paloma, which leveled the island in November 2008 (locals quip that all 18 churches sustained significant damage—but no bars).

Columbus first discovered the island by mistake during his final voyage in 1503; explorers and privateers made infrequent pit stops over the next three centuries, the Bluff serving as a vital navigational landmark. Though the Brac wasn't permanently settled until the 1830s, its short history seethes with dramatic incident, from marauding pirates to ravaging hurricanes. Today, despite its small size (roughly 12 miles by 1½ miles [19 km by 2½ km], or 14 square miles [36 square km]), the Brac is reinventing itself as an ecocentric adventure destination. Aside from the great dive sites, bonefish in the shallows and game fish in the deeper offshore waters lure anglers. The island hosts numerous ecosystems from arid semidesert stippled with cacti to ancient dry woodlands thick with exotic, fragrant flowers and trees. More than 200 bird species, both indigenous and migratory—including the endangered Cayman Brac parrot—flutter about. Nature trails filigree the interior, and several caves can be easily accessed. No surprise that the island is also considered one of the world's most exotic rock-climbing destinations, famous for its sheer vertical cliffs.

Hamlets with names like Watering Place, Cotton Tree Bay, Creek (Rock), and Spot Bay hold charming restored homes typical of seafaring architecture embroidered with carefully tended yards bursting with tropical blooms. Dozens of tiny churches line the road, bordered by sand graveyards. Despite the expats gradually boosting the year-round population, development remains as blissfully slow as the pace, though one longtime escapee from the stateside rat race grumbles about fancier cars and faster driving. There's still no stoplight, and traffic is defined by two locals stopping in the middle of the road to chat. It's as idyllic as a partially developed island can be. Indeed, the Brac is the affectionate butt of jokes from other Caymanians: "Two 60-year-old Brackers were so bored they decided to put in a bomb threat," starts one; the punch line is that they fall asleep first. Another refers to the three or four families dominating the phone book: "The most confusing day of the year on the Brac is Father's Day."

But Brackers take it all in stride, knowing their tranquil existence and abundant natural splendors give them the last laugh in the tourism sweepstakes.

Planning

Getting Here and Around

AIR

Cayman Airways Express provides Twin Otter service several times daily from Grand Cayman to Cayman Brac. There's also direct service from Miami on larger aircraft. Depending on the flight route, you may land on Little Cayman first. The flight is approximately 40 minutes nonstop. Cayman Brac has its own small airport, Sir Captain Charles Kirkconnell International Airport (CYB).

CAR

You need a car to really explore Cayman Brac, though hotels often provide complimentary bikes. Your own valid driver's license allows you to drive for up to six months in the Cayman Islands. Rental cars range from $35 to $55 per day depending on the type and size of the vehicle.

Driving is on the left. Gasoline is expensive; there are only two stations (one at each end of the island), and hours can be erratic. The main road circumnavigating the island and the bypass over the Bluff connecting the north and south coasts are well maintained. Yellow lines on roads indicate no parking zones. Most locals park on the side of the road.

Four D's, which carries mostly Nissans, tends to have cheaper rates, but rarely offers discounts. B&S Motor Ventures offers compacts, midsize vehicles, jeeps, SUVs, and vans. The only on-site airport agency, CB Rent-A-Car, has Honda, Hyundai, and Toyota vehicles, from compact cars to minivans. Most agencies offer a low-season discount and/or complimentary pickup and drop-off.

CONTACTS B&S Motor Ventures. ⚓ *Within walking distance of Cayman Brac Beach Resort, Brac Caribbean Beach Villas, and Carib Sands* ☎ *345/948–1646* ⊕ *www.bandsmv.com.* **CB Rent-A-Car.** ✉ *Airport Dr., Gerrard Smith Airport, West End* ☎ *345/948–2424, 345/948–2847* ⊕ *www.cbrent-a-car.com.* **Four D's Car Rental.** ✉ *Kidco Bldg., Bert Marson Dr.* ☎ *345/948–1599, 345/948–0459.*

TAXI

Brackers often wear several hats, so your taxi driver might also turn into your tour guide, who might also take you out fishing or serve you drinks; all of the local drivers are fonts of local lore and legend. An island day tour generally costs $25 per person, with a minimum of two people. Occasionally, you may have to wait to be picked up. Your hotel can arrange airport transfers. Rates are generally fixed: $8 to the closest hotels like Cayman Brac Beach Resort, $15 to Cayman Breakers near the southeastern tip, $20 to the Bight and Spot Bay on the north side. Drivers will generally load up passengers from several properties, including individual villas.

The tourist office and the hotels have a list of preferred providers, all Brackers who can regale you with stories of their upbringing.

Hotels

Cayman Brac currently has just one full-scale resort, as well as several apartments. Several private villas on Cayman Brac can also be rented, most of them basic but well maintained, ranging from one to four bedrooms. The rental fees are quite reasonable, and normally the price for extra couples in the larger units is only $200 per week (singles $100–$135, children often free), representing substantial savings for families or couples traveling together, while the kitchen helps reduce the price of dining out. In addition, government tax and often a service fee are sometimes included in the quoted rate (be sure to verify this), and most villa owners arrange a 10% discount with car-rental agencies. As a general rule of thumb, properties are thoroughly cleaned before your arrival; you must pay extra if you want daily maid service, and a one-time cleaning fee of $50 to $75 is usually assessed for end-of-rental cleaning. Owners can sometimes arrange to stock the fridge before your arrival. Each villa has a manager who must meet you at the airport (or car-rental agency), then escort you to your home; you'll be provided with his or her contact information during the reservation process. Rates are sometimes discounted in the off-season. Contact the tourist office for information.

Most villa owners mandate a three- to seven-night minimum stay in high season (assume at least one week's booking during the Christmas holiday unless otherwise noted), though this is often negotiable. Some owners will leave a kayak or snorkeling gear out for guests' use. If such amenities are included, they're mentioned. Unless otherwise noted, properties have landlines; local calls are usually free, but phones are generally locked for international calls. If your GSM provider works in the Cayman Islands, activate the international capability, but note that service is poor or nonexistent at some villas on the south side beneath the Bluff.

Hotel reviews have been shortened. For full information, visit Fodors.com.

What It Costs in U.S. Dollars			
$	$$	$$$	$$$$
RESTAURANTS			
under $12	$12–$20	$21–$30	over $30
HOTELS			
under $275	$275–$375	$376–$475	over $475

Restaurants

Most resorts offer optional meal plans, but there are several independent restaurants on the island, some of which provide free transport from your hotel. Local restaurants serve island fare (local seafood, chicken, and curries, as well as addictive beef patties). On Friday and Saturday night the spicy scent of jerk chicken fills the air; several roadside stands sell take-out dinners. Look for the local specialty, a sweetish, pillow-soft, round bread.

Visitor Information

From 8:30 to 5 pm on weekdays, the affable staff at the Sister Islands office of the Cayman Islands Department of Tourism can supply brochures on accommodations, dive outfits, activities, and nature and heritage trails. This office also services Little Cayman.

CONTACTS Cayman Islands Department of Tourism. ✉ 209 West End Community Park, West End ☎ 345/948–1649 ⊕ www.visitcaymanislands.com.

What to Read

Ian Stewart wrote a fine article on Brac climbing for the website of the Sister Islands Department of Tourism (⊕ www.caymanbrac.com/islandattractions/climbing.html). The **J. W. Harper blog** also contains useful links (⊕ www.skipharper.com). Though some of these articles and trip reports were written a few years ago, they're still pertinent. A more regularly updated blog devoted to the destination is ⊕ www.climbcaymanbrac.com.

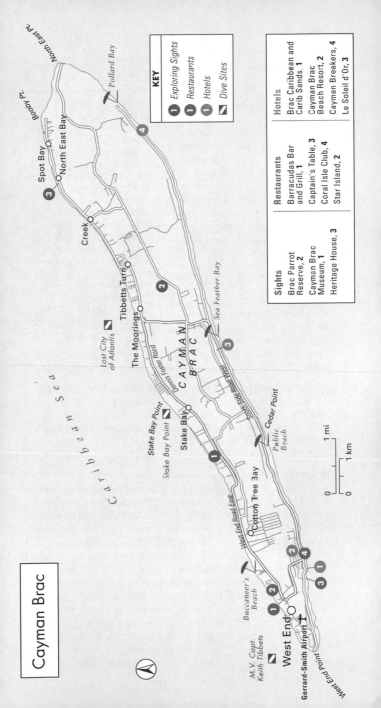

Cayman Brac

KEY

- **1** Exploring Sights
- **1** Restaurants
- **1** Hotels
- ◪ Dive Sites

Sights

Brac Parrot Reserve, **2**
Cayman Brac Museum, **1**
Heritage House, **3**

Restaurants

Barracudas Bar and Grill, **1**
Captain's Table, **3**
Coral Isle Club, **4**
Star Island, **2**

Hotels

Brac Caribbean and Carib Sands, **1**
Cayman Brac Beach Resort, **2**
Cayman Breakers, **4**
Le Soleil d'Or, **3**

0 1 mi
0 1 km

Caribbean Sea

North East Pt.
Pollard Bay
Booby Pt.
Spot Bay
North East Bay
Creek
Tibbetts Turn
The Moorings
Lost City of Atlantis
Stake Bay Point
Stake Bay
Dennis Foster Road
Sea Feather Bay
CAYMAN BRAC
South Side Road West
Cedar Point
Public Beach
Cotton Tree Bay
West End Road East
Buccaneer's Beach
West End
M.V. Capt. Keith Tibbetts
Gerrard-Smith Airport
West End Point

◉ Sights

The Brac abounds in both natural and historic attractions. Many of the former include botanic gardens and preserves set aside to protect threatened indigenous species. The latter revolve around the maritime heritage and hardscrabble lives of the earliest settlers and their descendants up until the island developed better communication with the outside world in the 1970s. *For more specific listings of caves and nature trails of particular significance, see Activities.*

If you're exploring on your own, be sure to pick up the *Cayman Brac Heritage Sites & Trails* brochure, available at the tourist office and most hotels; it lists all the major points of interest.

Caymanite

Found only in the crevices of the Bluff, this stone is actually an amalgam of several metals and minerals, including magnesium, iron, calcium, sodium, copper, nickel, phosphorus, and more—practically a quarter of the periodic table. Its striations supposedly represent different geologic eras, ranging from russet to white; no two pieces are identical. Special tools including diamond-tipped cutting wheels and grinders hone the extremely hard rock to a dazzling marble-like finish.

The **Sister Islands District Administration** (☎ *345/948–2222, ask for organizer Chevala Burke* ⊕ *www.naturecayman.com*) offers free government-sponsored guided nature and cultural tours with trained local guides Cantrell Scott and Keino Daley. Options include the Parrot Reserve, nature trails, wetlands, Lighthouse/Bluff View, caving, birding, and heritage sites.

★ Brac Parrot Reserve

NATURE PRESERVE | The likeliest place to spot the endangered Cayman Brac parrot—and other indigenous and migratory birds—is along this National Trust hiking trail off Major Donald Drive, aka Lighthouse Road. Prime time is early morning or late afternoon; most of the day they're camouflaged by trees, earning them the moniker "stealth parrot." The loop trail incorporates part of a path the Brackers used in olden days to cross the bluff to reach their provision grounds on the south shore or to gather coconuts, once a major export crop. It passes through several types of terrain: old farmland under grass and native trees from mango to mahogany unusually mixed with orchids and cacti. Wear sturdy shoes, as the terrain is rocky, uneven, and occasionally rough. The 6-mile (10-km) gravel road continues to the lighthouse at the bluff's eastern end, where there's an astonishing view from atop the cliff to the open ocean—the best place to watch the sunrise. ⊠ *Lighthouse Rd., Tibbetts Turn* ✛ *½ mile (1 km) south of town* ☎ *345/948–0319* 🎫 *Free.*

Cayman Brac Museum

MUSEUM | A diverse, well-displayed collection of historic Bracker implements ranges from dental pliers to pistols to pottery. A meticulously crafted scale model of the Caymanian catboat *Alsons* has pride of place. The front room reconstructs the Customs, Treasury, bank, and post office as they looked decades ago. Permanent exhibits include those on the 1932 hurricane, turtling, shipbuilding, and old-time home life. The back room hosts rotating exhibits such as one on herbal folk medicine. ⊠ *Old Government Administration Bldg., Stake Bay* ☎ *345/948–2622, 345/244–4446* 🎫 *Free.*

Heritage House

ARTS VENUE | An acre of beautifully landscaped grounds dotted with thatched gazebos and fountains includes an old-fashioned well and tannery as well as Cola Cave (used to shelter the former estate owners during hurricanes), with informational panels. The main building, though new, replicates a traditional house; the interior has a few displays and videos depicting Brac history, but the most fascinating element is watching local artists at work. It's a great resource for books on natural history and Caymanian crafts. Daily slide shows, various cultural events, and talks by visiting naturalists are often scheduled. Call before visiting to make sure that the house is open. ⊠ *218 N.E. Bay Rd., Spot Bay* ☎ *345/948–0563* 🎫 *Free.*

Beaches

Much of the Brac's coastline is ironshore, though there are several pretty sand beaches, mostly along the southwest coast (where swimmers will also find extensive beds of turtle grass, which creates less than ideal conditions for snorkeling). In addition to the hotel beaches, where everyone is welcome, there is a public beach with good access to the reef; it's well marked on tourist maps. The north-coast beaches, predominantly rocky ironshore, offer excellent snorkeling.

Buccaneer's Beach

BEACH—SIGHT | Just north of the airport, the rocky stretch is somewhat rough, but the snorkeling is sublime; you'll recognize the area when you see the 1860 windlass (winch) of the SS *Kersearge* in the ironshore. **Amenities:** none. **Best for:** snorkeling. ⊠ *Georgiana Dr., West End* ✛ *Just before North Side Rd. E.*

Did You Know?

The Cayman Brac parrot is an endangered species, but you may see one if you visit the Parrot Reserve.

Pollard Bay

BEACH—SIGHT | The beach by Cayman Breakers is fairly wide for this eastern stretch of the island. Start clambering east underneath the imposing bluff, past the end of the paved road, to strikingly beautiful deserted stretches accessible only on foot. The water here starts churning like a washing machine and becomes progressively rockier, littered with driftwood. Locals search for whelks here. Steps by the Breakers lead to shore dive sites. Flocks of seabirds darken the sun for seconds at a time, while blowholes spout as if answering migrant humpback whales. Don't go beyond the gargantuan rock called First Cay— the sudden swells can be hazardous—unless you're a serious rock climber. **Amenities:** none. **Best for:** solitude; walking. ⊠ *South Side Rd. E, East End.*

The Great Hurricane of '32 👁

Brackers were ill prepared for the 200 mph hurricane winds that blustered their way over the island in 1932, destroying virtually everything in their path. Most Brackers took shelter in the caves sculpted from the Bluff. Others flooded into the Spellman-McLaughlin home, which miraculously stood fast, saving 130 people. A "tear of sea" (archaic argot for a tidal wave) crashed onto shore, sending a boulder hurtling through the front door. Other than some damage from flooding, the house withstood the brunt of the storm, and even the windows remained unbroken. Even younger Brackers still discuss the storm with awe, though Paloma in 2008 matched its fury.

Public Beach

BEACH—SIGHT | Roughly 2 miles (3 km) east of the Brac Reef and Carib Sands/Brac Caribbean resorts, just past the wetlands (the unsightly gate is visible from the road; if you hit the Bat Cave you've passed it), lie a series of strands culminating in this beach, relatively deserted despite its name. The surf is calm and the crystalline water fairly protected for swimming. There are picnic tables and showers in uncertain condition. Snorkeling is quite good. **Amenities:** showers. **Best for:** snorkeling. ⊠ *South Side Rd. W.*

Sea Feather Bay

BEACH—SIGHT | The central section of the south coast features several lengthy ribbons of soft ecru sand, only occasionally maintained, with little shade aside from the odd coconut palm, no facilities, and blissful privacy (aside from some villas). **Amenities:** none. **Best for:** solitude; swimming, walking. ⊠ *South Side Rd., just west of Ashton Reid Dr., Sea Feather Bay.*

🍴 Restaurants

While there aren't many full-service restaurants (apart from those at the resorts), most of the island's bars also serve food (some of it quite good). *See Nightlife for more recommendations.*

Barracudas Bar and Grill

$$ | AMERICAN | You'll find happy locals mingling with island visitors at this friendly place with a fun atmosphere, working a/c (not a given on this island), delicious cocktails, ice-cold beers, and welcoming bartenders. It's locally famous for its wood-burning oven and New York–style pizzas, live music, and domino games. **Known for:** wood-oven pizzas; lively atmosphere; cocktails. ⑤ *Average main: $15* ⊠ *West End* ☎ *345/948–8511.*

Captain's Table

$$ | EUROPEAN | This weathered, powder-blue, wooden building wouldn't be out of place on some remote New England shore, except perhaps for the garish pirate at the entrance. The nautical yo-ho-hokum continues inside—painted oars, model sailboats, and droll touches like a skeleton with a chef's toque—but fortunately the kitchen isn't lost at sea, despite voyaging from India to Italy. **Known for:** "honey-stung" chicken; shoot the breeze with locals and dive crew; nautical decor. ⑤ *Average main: $19* ⊠ *Brac Caribbean, 165 South Side Rd.* ☎ *345/948–1418.*

Coral Isle Club

$$ | CARIBBEAN | This seaside eatery daubed in a virtual rainbow of blues from turquoise to teal serves up fine local food, emphasizing fresh seafood and, on weekends, mouth- and eye-watering barbecue. The lusciously painted outdoor bar offers equally colorful sunsets, cocktails, and characters (one regular swears, "If I were any better, I'd be dangerous," before buying another round). **Known for:** fun local clientele; mouthwatering barbecue; weekend entertainment. ⑤ *Average main: $18* ⊠ *Off South Side Rd., West End* ☎ *345/948–2500.*

Star Island

$$ | CARIBBEAN | Offering dine-in and take-out options, this popular spot has an almost endless and diverse menu that includes Caribbean cuisine like oxtail, plantains, and rice and beans as well as the national dish, turtle stew. With friendly, attentive staff and a cozy, American diner atmosphere, it's a big hit with both locals and visitors. **Known for:** Caribbean cuisine; laid-back atmosphere; conch fritters and coconut cream pie. ⑤ *Average main: $15* ⊠ *West Side Rd., West End* ☎ *345/948–8406.*

Hotels

Brac Caribbean and Carib Sands

$ | **RESORT** | These neighboring, beachfront sister complexes offer condos with one to four bedrooms, all individually owned and decorated. **Pros:** lively restaurant-bar; weekly discounts excellent value for families; reasonably priced for beachfront property. **Cons:** narrow unmaintained beach; limited staff; Wi-Fi dodgy. ⑤ *Rooms from: $190* ⊠ *Bert Marson Dr.* ☎ *345/948–2265, 866/843–2722, 345/948–1121, 864/498–4206 toll-free* ⊕ *www.braccaribbean.ky, www.caribsands.com* ⬔ *65 condos* ⦿ *No meals.*

Cayman Brac Beach Resort

$$ | **RESORT** | Popular with divers, this well-run ecofriendly resort features a beautiful sandy beach shaded by seagrape trees slung with hammocks and a sizable free-form pool. **Pros:** great dive outfit; coin-operated laundry on-site; free Wi-Fi. **Cons:** noise from planes; view often obscured from ground-floor units; rates include breakfast and dinner, but mandatory airport transfer of $20 per person extra. ⑤ *Rooms from: $340* ⊠ *West End* ☎ *345/948–1323, 727/308–7474 for reservations in Florida, 855/484–0808* ⊕ *www.caymanbracbeachresort.com* ⬔ *40 rooms* ⦿ *Free Breakfast.*

Cayman Breakers

$ | **RENTAL** | This attractive, pink-brick, colonnaded condo development sitting between the bluff and the southeast coastal ironshore caters to climbers, who scale the bluff's sheer face, as well as divers, who appreciate the good shore diving right off the property. **Pros:** spectacular views; thoughtful extras like complimentary bikes, jigsaw puzzles, and climbing-route guides; very attentive managers who live on-site. **Cons:** nearest grocery is a 15-minute drive; gorgeous beach is rocky with rough surf; some units slightly musty and faded. ⑤ *Rooms from: $175* ⊠ *The Moorings, 1902 South Side Rd. E, near East End* ☎ *345/948–1463, 345/927–8826* ⬔ *26 condos* ⦿ *No meals* ⌗ *3-night minimum stay.*

Le Soleil d'Or

$$ | **HOTEL** | With its lush grounds and a rugged coastline as a backdrop, Le Soleil d'Or calls itself as "a Caribbean Farm Inn," and that's exactly what it is. **Pros:** beach views; farm-to-table dining; peaceful atmosphere. **Cons:** not for those who want a lively atmosphere; restaurant is pricey; activities not included. ⑤ *Rooms from: $310* ⊠ *2147 South Side Rd., Sea Feather Bay* ☎ *345/948–0555* ⊕ *www.lesoleildor.com* ⬔ *8 rooms* ⦿ *Free Breakfast.*

House of Worship

The pale blue, circular Temple Beth Shalom nestles incongruously in the serene garden of the now-shuttered Walton's Mango Manor in Stake Bay, replete with the only consecrated Jewish cemetery in the Cayman Islands. A plaque by the imposing carved mahogany door reads "House of Welcome, May All Who Enter Here Find Peace." Rabbis and cantors sometimes fly in for special occasions and holidays.

Swiss architect Fredy Schulteiss designed the building, but George and Lynne Walton practically built it by themselves. It includes stained glass, Italian marble accents from Italy, and polished gray Minnesota granite floors they laid themselves. Lynne carved everything from the marble to the Honduran mahogany doors and inlaid scrolling fashioned from dead limbs of wild plum, cedar, mahogany, ironwood, and candlewood trees. Her father created a menorah in the shape of a shofar; another was a family heirloom brought by Lynne's grandmother from Odessa. The synagogue is actually one structure encased within another, "one for the Torah, the other to reach toward the heavens, in a small way making a statement to God that we're trying to get there." The 28-foot ceiling fittingly depicts a starry sky, with the 12 lights representing the 12 tribes of Israel. As a bonus, the space has splendid acoustics and a piano. Members of the Cayman National Orchestra, including flutists, pianists, and cellists, occasionally perform memorable classical concerts.

Nightlife

Divers are notoriously early risers, but a few bars keep things hopping if not quite happening, especially on weekends, when local bands (or "imports" from Grand Cayman) often perform. Quaintly reminiscent of *Footloose* (without the hellfire and brimstone), watering holes are required to obtain music and dancing permits. Various community events including talent shows, recitals, concerts, and other stage presentations at the Aston Rutty Centre provide the rest of the island's nightlife.

Barracuda's Bar

BARS/PUBS | New Yorker Terry Chesnard built his dream bar from scratch, endowing it with an almost 1960s Rat Pack ambience. Nearly everything is handcrafted, from the elegant bar itself to the blown-glass light fixtures to the drinks. Try the Barracuda shot special "if you dare," or the cocktails, though Terry takes the greatest pride in his top-of-the-line espresso machine. The kitchen elevates pub grub to an art form with pizzas, Reubens, and French melts. Locals flock here for free pasta Friday, karaoke Wednesday, and live music on Thursday. You might walk in on a hotly contested darts, shuffleboard, or dominoes tournament, but the vibe is otherwise mellow at this charming time-warp hangout. ☒ *20 West End Rd., Creek* ☎ *345/948–8511.*

La Esperanza

BARS/PUBS | Known islandwide as Bussy's after the larger-than-life owner, La Esperanza overflows with drinks and good cheer. On weekends, seemingly half the island can be found here, when Bussy fires up the grill and hosts a huge beach jerk barbecue (he'll occasionally give impromptu jerk lessons). Shoot pool in the colorful lounge, or pass time at the alfresco bar or the covered pier jutting into the Caribbean. Drink in the sunset views (and cocktails in matching colors), and if available, try the luscious key lime pie made by Bussy's wife, Velma. The music, heavy on the reggae with the occasional salsa tune thrown in, blares, encouraging everyone to sway along. ☒ *The Creek, Stake Bay* ☎ *345/948–0591.*

Pat's Kitchen

BARS/PUBS | Pat's (previously Bucky's) is popular for its all-you-can-eat West Indian lunch buffets. But the real allure is free Wi-Fi and the cushy (if frayed) lounge adjacent to the restaurant, which resembles a small Vegas sports bar with leather armchairs, black-and-white photos, and team pennants and jerseys galore. Open until 11 pm. ☒ *227 West End Rd., West End* ☎ *345/929–8253.*

Tipsy Turtle Pub

BARS/PUBS | This pub overflows with good cheer and strong drinks. The mudslides are particularly potent, and there are usually some good Cubanos. The alfresco, split-level bar (great water views from the top) serves excellent pub grub (jerk chicken pizza, Caesar salad wrap, portobello-and-Swiss cheeseburger, messy and marvelous spare ribs, tempura shrimp) for around $10 a dish. It's the kind of casual congenial hangout where almost everyone ends up buying a round at some point. Stop by for Tuesday bingo, Wednesday karaoke, or Friday barbecue with live music, which attracts large, enthusiastic crowds. ☒ *Cayman Brac Beach Resort, West End* ☎ *345/948–1323.*

Vibrant living reefs help make Cayman Brac one of the world's best diving destinations.

Shopping

Shopping is limited on the Brac; there are a few small stores, though some locals sell their wares from home. You'll also find a boutique at the Cayman Brac Beach Resort. Specialty crafts here are woven-thatch items and Caymanite jewelry.

Kirkconnell's Market

FOOD/CANDY | Located near Cedar point, this grocery store offers a large selection of fresh food, dairy, frozen food, and household items. It also holds the flagship branch for Digicel Cayman Brac, with a wide range of phones, phone accessories, and phone cards for sale. ⊠ *211 Stake Bay Rd., Stake Bay* ☎ *345/948–2252*.

★ NIM Things

JEWELRY/ACCESSORIES | Artist and raconteur Tenson Scott fashions exquisite jewelry from Caymanite (he climbs down from the lighthouse without ropes to chisel the stone), triton shells, sea eggs, and more unusual materials—hence the name, which stands for Native Island Made. His wife, Starrie, creates delicate works from sea urchins, hardening the shell with epoxy: cute turtles, bud vases, and planters decorated with minuscule shells. ⊠ *N.E. Bay Rd., Spot Bay* ☎ *345/948–0461, 345/939–5306*.

Treasure Chest

CLOTHING | The shop carries simple resort wear, T-shirts, bonnets, handbags (usually with the Brac logo), and black coral and Caymanite jewelry, as well as a small selection of books, including

Thatch Weaving

"Laying rope" is an old-time tradition that originated so that women could support themselves while the men were away at sea, often for months at a time. The Brac was particularly noted for the method of stripping silver thatch palm leaves and drying them in the sun, both creating a labor-intensive twisted hemplike rope that was exported to Jamaica, usually in barter, and various baskets for carrying sand (for gardens) and provisions from little farms atop the Bluff.

You can visit the home studio/shop of the craft's foremost practitioner, **Annelee Ebanks** (⊠ 35 White Bay Rd., West End ☎ 345/948–1326), whose skill is such that the Ritz-Carlton commissions her to create pieces as gifts, decorative accents, towel hampers, and waste baskets. Miss Annelee began more than half a century ago at 13 watching her father make traditional baskets.

The stripped dried thatch "strings" have several gradations in hue from silvery mint to buff; bunches are tied off in places to ensure the sun doesn't bleach out all the color. She also uses darker brown dried stripped coconut leaves to create multicolored pieces: place mats with matching coasters and napkin rings, hats, baskets, purses, sandals, hand fans, even brooms and switches, since thatching originally served utilitarian purposes. It takes her three days to create one beach bag: one day to weave, a second to line and stitch, another to decorate (she uses Magic Marker and spray paint, as well as raffia from Jamaica for binding and decorative curlicues).

pamphlets on local birds and fish. ⊠ Tibbetts Sq., West End ☎ 345/948–1333.

Activities

BIRD-WATCHING

Bird-watching is sensational on the Sister Islands, with almost 200 species patrolling the island from migratory to endemic, including the endangered Cayman Brac parrot and brown booby. The best place to spy the feathered lovelies is on the north coast and in the protected woodland reserve (see Brac Parrot Reserve in Sights) on the Bluff. Other species to look out for include the indigenous vitelline warbler and red-legged thrush. The wetlands and ponds in the West End teem with herons and shorebirds, including splendid frigates, kestrels, ospreys, and rare West Indian whistling ducks. Most coastal areas offer sightings, but the best may be just inland at the **Westerly Ponds** (which connect during rainy season; otherwise boardwalks provide excellent viewing areas). A hundred species flap about, particularly around the easternmost pond off Bert Marson Drive by Mr. Billy's house: the old Bracker feeds them late afternoon and occasionally early morning, when the whistling ducks practically coat the entire surface of the water.

DIVING AND SNORKELING

Cayman Brac's waters are celebrated for their rich diversity of sea life, from hammerhead and reef sharks to stingrays to sea horses. Divers and snorkelers alike will find towering coral heads, impressive walls, and fascinating wrecks. The snorkeling and shore diving off the **north coast** are spectacular, particularly at West End, where nearby coral formations attract all kinds of critters. The walls feature remarkable topography with natural gullies, caves, and fissures blanketed with Technicolor sponges, black coral, gorgonians, and sea fans. Some of the famed sites are the West Chute, Cemetery Wall, Airport Wall, and Garden Eel Wall.

The **South Wall** is a wonderland of sheer drop-offs carved with a maze of vertical swim-throughs, tunnels, arches, and grottoes that divers nickname Cayman's Grand Canyon. Notable sites include Anchor Wall, Rock Monster Chimney, and the Wilderness.

Notable diving attractions around the island include the 330-foot MV *Capt. Keith Tibbetts,* a Russian frigate purchased from Cuba and deliberately scuttled in 1996 within swimming distance of the northwest shore, accessible to divers of all levels. Many fish have colonized the Russian frigate—now broken in two and encrusted with magnificent orange and yellow sponges. Other underwater wrecks include the *Cayman Mariner,* a steel tugboat, and the *Prince Frederick,* a wooden-hulled twin-masted schooner that allegedly sank in the 19th century.

Oceanic Voyagers, a 7-foot-tall bronze statue created by world-renowned marine sculptor Dale Evers, depicts spotted dolphins cavorting with southern stingrays. It was sunk off the Brac's coast near Stake Bay in January 2003 as part of the Cayman Islands' yearlong quincentennial celebration. An artist named Foots has created an amazing underwater Atlantis off Radar Reef.

Other top snorkeling/shore diving spots include the south coast's **Pillar Coral Reef, Tarpon Reef,** and **Lighthouse Reef**; the north shore counters with **Greenhouse Reef, Snapper Reef,** and **Jan's Reef.**

Brac Scuba Shack

DIVING/SNORKELING | Partners Martin van der Touw, wife Liesel, and Steve Reese form a tremendous troika at this PADI outfit, whose

selling points include small groups (10 divers max on the custom Newton 36), flexible departures, valet service, and computer profiles. The 30-foot central console *Big Blue* takes no more than five divers and does double-duty for deep-sea fishing. Courses range from Discover Scuba through Divemaster Training, as well as such specialties as wreck, nitrox, and night diving. Rates are par for the course ($110 for two-tank dives), but multiday discounts are available. ⊠ *West End* ☎ *345/948–8472, 345/925–3215 mobile* ⊕ *www.bracscubashack.com.*

Reef Divers

SCUBA DIVING | Pluses here include five Newton boats from 42 to 46 feet, valet service, and enthusiastic, experienced staff; slightly higher rates reflect the extras. Certified divers can purchase à la carte dive packages even if they aren't hotel guests. They also arrange snorkeling tours. ⊠ *Cayman Brac Beach Resort, West End* ☎ *345/948–1642, 345/948–1323* ⊕ *www.reefdiverscaymanbrac.com, www.caymanbracbeachresort.com.*

FISHING

Cayman Brac offers superior bonefishing along the shallows off the southwest coast and even finer light-tackle action. The offshore waters mostly compose a marine park, so fishers go out a few hundred feet from the dive buoys, themselves ranging ¼ to ½ mile (½ to 1 km) from shore. The pristine environment teems with wahoo, marlin, and sushi-grade tuna. Most charter-boat operators also run snorkeling trips; a memorable excursion is to Little Cayman Brac, passing several fanciful rock formations.

Robin Walton

FISHING | This experienced guide has been fishing the waters commercially for years and knows the best times and secret spots where mahimahi, wahoo, marlin, grouper, and tuna hang out. His 21-foot Bayliner Trophy, *TLC,* is equipped with GPS tracking, he quips, "because I'm lazy." He takes you to truly wonderful sites, since he doesn't like the dive-boat traffic. The maximum is four anglers, though he can fit up to eight comfortably for snorkeling. His rates are also fairly reasonable ($125 per hour) because you subsidize his income with your catch, though he generally allots 50% "or whatever you can manage" to his guests, most of whom cook at their rentals. ⊠ *Stake Bay* ☎ *345/948–2382, 345/925–2382.*

HIKING

Public footpaths and hiking trails filigree the island, with interpretive signs identifying a staggering variety of resident and nonresident bird species that call the Brac home. You'll also find reptile habitats, indigenous flora, and historically and geologically significant sites. Arguably the most scenic route traverses the

Sculpting Cayman

A Brac sculptor known as Foots (real name Ronald Kynes) for his size-16 feet, dreamed of re-creating Plato's lost city of Atlantis. Four decades later, he realized this dream by creating mammoth sculptures and sinking them 45 feet off the Brac's north shore. The resulting artificial reef is an astounding artistic achievement and engineering feat with more than 100 pieces covering several acres; even partial destruction by Hurricane Paloma didn't faze Foots.

An architect-contractor fascinated by ruins and mythology, Foots found his niche restoring historic buildings, including churches in Germany, Austria, and Iran. To secure permits, he submitted a video of his ideal site and a 140-page environmental impact report to the Department of the Environment, noting the goodwill and revenue it would generate in the scuba and tourism industries. "I have money, I just need your blessing," Foots wrote.

He has spent thousands of dollars ("What price making a dream come true?") and years of his life into the project, which launched officially in 2005, when 150,000 pounds of sculpture were submerged. Specially constructed barges helped position the pieces by cranes, lift bags, and drag floats. The technical marvel encompasses nearly 300,000 pounds. The scale is immense, but, as Foots says, "Hopes and dreams make the world livable … I'm promoting new life and marine growth through art that will last an eternity."

The story starts at the Archway of Atlantis (its two bases weigh 21,000 pounds each). The Elders' Way, lined with 5-foot temple columns, leads to the Inner Circle of Light, centering a 2,600-pound sundial. Two 50,000-pound pyramids tower 20 feet with eight swim-throughs. One ambitious project, the Colossus, a toppled 30-foot statue broken into pieces like 7-foot-long feet and a scepter, will suggest the Lost City's destruction.

Foots modeled the statues after actual people who have contributed to Cayman. He fashions exact plaster of paris molds of their faces (and sometimes hands), then casts in limestone-based cement. Copper piping and doorknobs ingeniously replicate papyrus scrolls; apothecary bottles complete the Medicine Men.

The project has continually evolved inside Foots's head since childhood, without architectural renderings: "I invent so many phases I'd never live long enough to finish… Atlantis will only end when I do."

eastern Bluff to the tip, where the remains of a lighthouse stand sentinel over the roaring Caribbean. This is one of the routes taken by early Brackers scaling the Bluff via the steep **Lighthouse Steps** up past Peter's Cave *(see Spelunking)*, then down the 2½-mile (4-km) **Lighthouse Footpath** adjacent to Major Donald Drive (aka Lighthouse Road). This was used to bring cattle to pasture, as well as to access plantations of cassava, peppers, beans, tomatoes, sweet potatoes, mangoes, bananas, and other crops. The panoramas are awe inspiring, especially once you reach the lighthouse. Even though the path along the edge is fairly even, it's not suitable for the elderly, very young, or infirm due to high winds (don't venture onto the dramatic bleached limestone outcroppings: a sudden gust could send you hurtling into the air with the brown boobies that nest in ledges and caves here). It's a compellingly desolate, eerie area, as if future spacefarers were terra-forming the moon with hardy "maypole" cacti, century plants, aloes, and wind-lashed silver thatch palms bowing almost as if in deference to nature.

Brac Tourism Office

HIKING/WALKING | Free printed guides to the Brac's many heritage and nature trails can be obtained here (and from the airport and hotels). Traditional routes across the bluff have been marked, as are trailheads along the road. It's safe to hike on your own, though some trails are fairly hard going (wear light hiking boots) and others could be better maintained. ✉ *West End Community Park, west of airport* ☎ *345/948–1649* ⊕ *www.itsyourstoexplore.com.*

Christopher Columbus Gardens

HIKING/WALKING | For those who prefer less-strenuous walking, these gardens have easy trails and boardwalks. The park showcases the unique natural flora and features of the bluff, including two cave mouths. This is a peaceful spot dotted with gazebos and wooden bridges comprising several ecosystems from cacti to mahogany trees. ✉ *Ashton Reid Dr. (Bluff Rd.), just north of Ashton Rutty Centre.*

Sister Islands District Administration

HIKING/WALKING | The administration arranges free, government-sponsored, guided nature and cultural tours with trained local guides. Options include the Parrot Reserve, nature trails, wetlands, Lighthouse/Bluff View, caving, birding, and heritage sites. ☎ *345/948–2222.*

ROCK CLIMBING

Aficionados consider the Brac among the world's leading exotic climbing destinations. If you are experienced and like dangling from ropes 140 feet above a rocky, churning sea, this is the place for you. Unfortunately, if you want to learn the ropes, no organization promotes climbing, though a new service rents equipment such as ropes and safety gear. Through the years, climbers have attached permanent titanium bolts to the **Bluff** face, creating some 70 routes in seven prime regions around the East End, most notably the Spot Bay areas, the North Wall, the East Wall, and the South Wall. Access is often via private property, so be respectful (though most Brackers will just invite you in for cold drinks and stimulating conversation). The number is still growing as aficionados create new ascents. Difficulty is high; the "easiest" routes are graded 5.8 by the Yosemite Decimal System; most are rated 5.10 to 5.12, though many experienced climbers argue some approach the dizzying 5.14 range, especially around the sheer, "pumpy" (rock-speak for adrenaline-flowing) Northeast Point. This is steep, gnarly terrain of varying stability, suitable only for experienced climbers. Most of the Bluff's faces are hard vertical to overhanging; many walls vault abruptly to the savage sea.

Climbing the Brac is exhilarating, but precautions are vital. Sturdy hiking boots are mandatory, since you'll traverse a wide variety of terrain just accessing routes. Leather gloves are also recommended, as most of the high-quality limestone is smooth but has sharp and jagged areas. Two ropes are necessary for many climbs, the longest of which requires 19 quickdraws. Gear should include ascending devices like prusiks and Tiblocs and shoulder-length slings with carabiners. Don't attempt climbs alone. Establish rope tug signals, as the wind, waves, and overhangs make hearing difficult. Always analyze surf conditions and prevailing winds (which are variable) before rappelling, and double-check rap setup, anchors, and harnesses. Though titanium glue-ins replaced most of the old stainless steel bolts, many are deteriorating due to stress corrosion cracking; avoid any old bolts.

The Cayman Breakers condo complex has route maps and descriptions *(see Where to Stay)*. Several world-renowned climbers have built (second) homes on the Brac, including Liz Grenard, John Byrnes, and Ian Stewart.

Rock Iguana

CLIMBING/MOUNTAINEERING | This company, run by world-class climbers, operates out of a mobile van, taking aficionados and amateurs alike to the Brac's best sites. They offer both instruction and top-notch gear (they've also been upgrading the bolts around the island). Rock Iguana can accommodate most requests, whether your thrill is rappelling down a sheer rock face or squeezing through barely accessible caverns carved into the bluff. Tours begin at $145 per person; instruction for all levels is $450 for two intense days. ☎ *345/936–2722* ⊕ *climb.ky*.

SPELUNKING

Residents and geologists are still discovering "new" caves and sinkholes in the Brac's 25- to 30-million-year-old dolomite rock. Most of these caves were formed when the sea receded after the last Ice Age. Rainwater dissolved the carbonate rock over millennia through cracks made by plants rooting in the limestone. Mineral deposits fashioned fanciful formations in many caves, as well as more typical pillars, stalagmites, and daggerlike stalactites.

Buccaneers (supposedly including Henry Morgan and Edward "Blackbeard" Teach) of the 17th and 18th centuries stopped like most mariners at the Cayman Islands to restock stores of water, wood, and turtles. Many locals still believe buried treasure lies deep within the recesses of the Bluff. But more vitally, the caves served as shelter during the fearsome storms of the first part of the 20th century.

Most caves are closed to the public—even to experienced spelunkers—but several are easily accessed and considered safe. If you plan to explore Cayman Brac's caves, wear good sneakers or hiking shoes, as some paths are steep and rocky and some entrances reachable only by ladders.

Peter's Cave offers a stunning aerial view of the picturesque northeastern community of Spot Bay. The climb is easier from atop the Bluff; the other access is steep, and purchase isn't always easy even with railings. The chambers feature few formations but some pretty multihue striations. **Great Cave,** at the island's southeast end, has numerous chambers and photogenic ocean views. It's the least accessible yet most impressive. You won't fund Bruce Wayne or his Boy Wonder in the **Bat Cave,** but you may see Jamaican fruit bats hanging from the ceiling (try not to disturb them), as well as nesting barn owls. The bats play a crucial role in the ecosystem's food chain because they devour overripe fruits, thereby pollinating plants, disseminating seeds, and reducing insect pests. There are some whimsical formations, and sections cracked and crawling with undergrowth, trees, and epiphytes. **Rebecca's Cave** houses the graveside of an 18-month-old child who died during the horrific hurricane of 1932. A plaque commemorates her short life ("Daughter of Raib and Helena 'Miss Missy' Bodden"), and people still leave flowers. It's actually a ¼-mile (½-km) hike inland along a well-marked trail called the Saltwater Pond Path, which continues to the north side. Today it's a prime bird-watching walk lined with indigenous flora like red birch, jasmine, silver thatch palms, agave, dildo cactus, balsam, cabbage trees, duppy bushes, and bull hoof plants.

Chapter 8

LITTLE CAYMAN

Updated by
Monica Walton

☉ Sights	🍴 Restaurants	🛏 Hotels	🛍 Shopping	🍸 Nightlife
★★★★☆	★★★★★	★★★★★	★★★☆☆	★★★☆☆

WELCOME TO LITTLE CAYMAN

TOP REASONS TO GO

★ **Wall-to-wall fun.** Divers can't miss the hallowed Bloody Bay, lauded by every Cousteau worth his sea salt.

★ **Bird-watching.** Even if you're not a birder, learning about the rare red-footed booby from its fanatics at the National Trust and spying them through telescopes are more fun than you'd think.

★ **Beachcombing.** A jaunt to Owen Island or Point of Sand rewards you with practically virgin strands, breathtaking views, and scintillating snorkeling.

★ **Something fishy.** The deep-sea fishing is superior, but the light-tackle option should lure any angler.

1 Blossom Village. A small village right next to the Little Cayman airport, it's where you'll find the island's only grocery store, and it's close to the Little Cayman Beach Resort. It was first established by a few families, mostly with the surname Bawden or Bodden, Scotts, and Ritch, who are said to have been part of Cromwell's army in Jamaica.

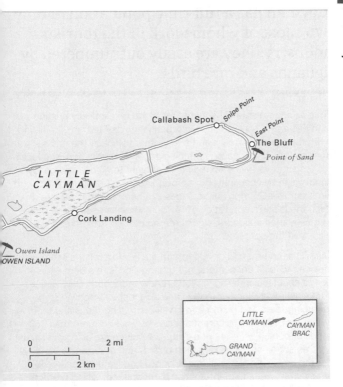

Callabash Spot — Snipe Point

East Point

The Bluff

Point of Sand

LITTLE CAYMAN

Cork Landing

Owen Island

OWEN ISLAND

| 0 | | 2 mi |
| 0 | 2 km | |

LITTLE CAYMAN — CAYMAN BRAC

GRAND CAYMAN

2 Head of Bay. With stunning panoramas and shallow waters, the bay is located on private property, though you are free to relax on the deck or in one of the hammocks and enjoy the breathtaking view of the beautiful, crystal clear Caribbean sea.

3 North Side. The most popular of the island's dive sites, Bloody Bay and Jackson's Bight, are both located here on the north side of the island, just west of the island's midpoint.

4 Preston Bay. This area lies on the south reef-protected coast of Little Cayman. There's great snorkeling and fishing straight out in front.

5 South Hole Sound. From this bay in the southwest corner of Little Cayman, you can kayak, boat or even swim to Owen Island. The area is also home to the National Trust's 200-acre Booby Pond Nature Reserve.

The smallest and most tranquil of the three inhabited Cayman Islands, Little Cayman has a full-time population of only 170, most of whom work in the tourism industry; they are easily outnumbered by iguanas and rare birds.

This 12-square-mile (31-square-km) island is practically pristine and has only a sand-sealed airstrip, sharing its "terminal" building with the fire department and a few other vehicles. The grass runway was finally paved with blacktop a few years ago, and locals no longer have to line up their cars at night to guide emergency landings in by headlight. But some things don't change. The speed limit remains 25 mph, as no one is in a hurry to go anywhere. In fact, the island's population of resident iguanas uses roads more regularly than residents; signs created by local artists read "Iguanas have the right of way."

With little commercial development, the island beckons ecotourists seeking wildlife encounters, not urban wild life. It's best known for its spectacular diving in world-renowned Bloody Bay Marine Park, including Bloody Bay Wall and adjacent Jackson Wall. The ravishing reefs and plummeting walls encircling the island teem with more than 500 different species of fish and more than 150 kinds of coral. Fly-, lake-, and deep-sea fishing are also popular, as well as snorkeling, kayaking, and biking. And the island's certainly for the birds. The National Trust Booby Pond Nature Reserve is a designated wetland of international importance, which protects around 20,000 red-footed boobies, the Western Hemisphere's largest colony. It's just one of many superlative spots to witness avian aerial acrobatics.

Secluded beaches, unspoiled tropical wilderness and wetlands, mangrove swamps, lagoons, bejeweled coral reefs—Little Cayman practically redefines "hideaway" and "escape." Yet aficionados appreciate that the low-key lifestyle doesn't mean sacrificing the high-tech amenities, and some of the resorts cater to a quietly wealthy yet unpretentious crowd.

Which isn't to say Little Cayman lacks for lively moments. Halloween parties and Mardi Gras festivities bring out wildly imaginative costumes and floats. It's just one of those rare places that attract more colorful types who are in search of privacy, not just the ardently ecocentric.

Planning

Getting Here and Around

AIR

Interisland service between Grand Cayman, Cayman Brac, and Little Cayman is provided several times daily by Cayman Airways at Edward Bodden Airfield, which accommodates only STOL craft.

CAR

Bikes, usually offered for free by the resorts, are the preferred way of getting around the island; dive operations will pick you up, and the hotels also provide airport transfers. A car is suggested only if you rent one of the more isolated villas or if you plan to explore the farther-flung part of the island on a regular basis. Parking is rarely a problem. Another flexible touring option is a moped. Little Cayman Car Rental offers mopeds ($50) and SUVs ($80–$100). There are also two scooter companies offering competitive rates.

CONTACTS Little Cayman Car Rental. ⊠ *898 Guy Banks Rd., Blossom Village* ☎ *345/948–1000* ✉ *littlcay@candw.ky.* **Scooten! Scooters!.** ☎ *345/916–4971* ⊕ *www.scootenscooters.com.*

TAXI

Resorts offer airport transfers. Most visitors get around by moped or car rental, which you can prearrange or book once you arrive on-island.

Hotels

Accommodations are mostly in small lodges, almost all of which offer meal and dive packages. The chefs in most places create wonderful meals despite often-limited resources. You won't find any independent restaurants, but if you are staying in a villa or condo you can usually have dinner at one of the resorts (be sure to call ahead). Dive packages represent exceptional savings. Most resorts prefer a five- to seven-night stay in high season, but the minimum isn't always strictly enforced. Still, rooms for shorter stays may not become available until two to three weeks prior to your trip dates.

Hotel reviews have been shortened. For full information, visit Fodors.com.

PRIVATE VILLAS

A few private villas on Little Cayman can be rented, most of them basic but well maintained, ranging from one to four bedrooms. There are also three condo complexes and one villa resort on the island. Rental fees are reasonable, and normally the price for extra couples in the larger units is only $200 per week, representing substantial savings for families or couples traveling together, while the kitchen helps reduce the price of dining out. In addition, government tax and often a service fee are sometimes included in the quoted rate (be sure to verify this). As a general rule of thumb, properties are thoroughly cleaned before your arrival; you must pay extra if you want daily maid service. Rates are sometimes discounted in the off-season. Most villa owners mandate a three- to seven-night minimum stay in high season, though this is often negotiable. Unless otherwise noted, properties have landline phones; local calls are usually free, but phones are generally locked for international calls.

HOTEL AND RESTAURANT PRICES

What It Costs in U.S. Dollars			
$	$$	$$$	$$$$
RESTAURANTS			
under $12	$12–$20	$21–$30	over $30
HOTELS			
under $275	$275–$375	$376–$475	over $475

Restaurants

The main all-inclusive resorts' dining rooms accept reservations from nonguests pending availability. Otherwise, there are other restaurants affiliated with villa/condo properties and the other resort, Southern Cross Club. The choices are limited, with seafood obviously reigning supreme, but the caliber of the few kitchens is generally high.

Visitor Information

There is no visitor center on Little Cayman, but each hotel, hotelier, and staffer overflows with information and suggestions. You can also consult the websites of the **Sister Islands Tourism Association** (⊕ *www.itsyourstoexplore.com*) for information on Little Cayman.

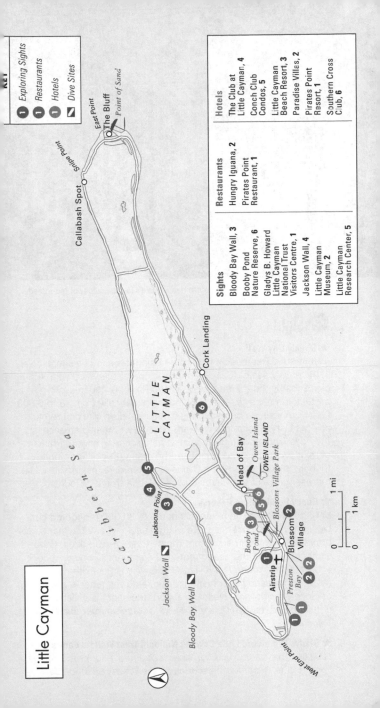

Little Cayman

Exploring Sights
Restaurants
Hotels
Dive Sites

West End Point
Bloody Bay Wall
Jackson Wall
Caribbean Sea
Jacksons Point
LITTLE CAYMAN
Snipe Point
Callabash Spot
East Point
The Bluff
Point of Sand
Cork Landing
Head of Bay
Owen Island
OWEN ISLAND
Blossom Village Park
Booby Pond
Preston Bay
Blossom Village
Airstrip

0   1 mi
0   1 km

Sights

Bloody Bay Wall, **3**
Booby Pond
Nature Reserve, **6**
Gladys B. Howard
Little Cayman
National Trust
Visitors Centre, **1**
Jackson Wall, **4**
Little Cayman
Museum, **2**
Little Cayman
Research Center, **5**

Restaurants

Hungry Iguana, **2**
Pirates Point
Restaurant, **1**

Hotels

The Club at
Little Cayman, **4**
Conch Club
Condos, **5**
Little Cayman
Beach Resort, **3**
Paradise Villas, **2**
Pirates Point
Resort, **1**
Southern Cross
Club, **6**

Little Cayman is home to the Western Hemisphere's largest colony of red-footed boobies, some 20,000 birds.

Sights

★ Bloody Bay Wall

NATURE SITE | This beach, named for being the site of a spectacular 17th-century sea battle, was declared one of the world's top three dive sites by the *maîtres* Jacques and Philippe Cousteau. Part of a protected marine reserve, it plunges dramatically from 18 to 6,000 feet, with a series of staggeringly beautiful drop-offs and remarkable visibility. Snorkelers who are strong swimmers can access the edge from shore, gliding among shimmering silver curtains of minnows, jacks, and bonefish. The creatures are amazingly friendly, including Jerry the Grouper, whom dive masters joke is a representative of the Cayman Islands Department of Tourism.

★ Booby Pond Nature Reserve

NATURE PRESERVE | The reserve is home to 20,000 red-footed boobies (the Western Hemisphere's largest colony) and Cayman's only breeding colony of magnificent frigate (man-of-war) birds. Other sightings include the near-threatened West Indian whistling duck and vitelline warbler. The RAMSAR Convention, an international treaty for wetland conservation, designated the reserve a wetland of global significance. Near the airport, the sanctuary also has a gift shop and reading library. ⊠ *Next to National Trust, Blossom Village.*

★ Gladys B. Howard Little Cayman National Trust Visitors Centre

COLLEGE | This traditional Caymanian cottage overlooks the Booby Pond Nature Reserve; telescopes on the breezy second-floor deck permit close-up views of their markings and nests, as well as other feathered friends. Inside are shell collections; panels and dioramas discussing endemic reptiles; models "in flight"; and diagrams on the growth and life span of red-footed boobies, frigate birds, egrets, and other island "residents." The shop sells exquisite jewelry made from Caymanite and spider-crab shells, extraordinary duck decoys and driftwood carvings, and great books on history, ornithology, and geology. Mike Vallee holds an iguana information session and tour every Friday at 4. The cheeky movie *Calendar Girls* inspired a local equivalent: women from Little Cayman going topless for an important cause—raising awareness of the red-footed booby and funds to purchase the sanctuary's land. Nicknamed, appropriately, "Support the Boobies," the calendar is tasteful, not titillating: the lasses strategically hold conch shells, brochures, flippers, tree branches, etc. ⊠ *Blossom Village* 🕾 *345/623–1107* ⊕ *www.nationaltrust.org.ky/little-cayman.*

★ Jackson Wall

REEF | Adjacent to Bloody Bay, Jackson Wall and reef are nearly as stunning. Conditions are variable, the water now glassy, now turbulent, so snorkelers must be strong swimmers. It's renowned for Swiss-cheese-like swim-throughs; though it's not as precipitous as Bloody Bay, the more rugged bottom results in astonishing rock formations whose tunnels and crevices hold pyrotechnic marine life.

Little Cayman Museum

MUSEUM | This gorgeously laid out and curated museum displays relics and artifacts, including one wing devoted to maritime memorabilia and another to superlative avian and marine photographs, which provide a good overview of this tiny island's history and heritage. ⊠ *Guy Banks Rd., across from Booby Pond Nature Reserve, Blossom Village* 🕾 *345/925–7625, 345/323–7166* ⊕ *www.littlecaymanmuseum.org* 🖃 *Free* 🕙 *Closed Sun.*

Little Cayman Research Center

COLLEGE | Near the Jackson Point Bloody Bay Marine Park reserve, this vital research center supports visiting students and researchers, with a long list of projects studying the biodiversity, human impact, reef health, and ocean ecosystem of Little Cayman. Reefs this unspoiled are usually far less accessible; the National Oceanic and Atmospheric Administration awarded it one of 16 monitoring stations worldwide. The center also solicits funding through the parent U.S. nonprofit organization Central Caribbean Marine Institute; if you value the health of our reefs, show your support on the website. Former chairman Peter Hillenbrand proudly calls it the "Ritz-Carlton of marine research facilities, which often are little more than pitched tents on a beach." Tours explain the center's mission and ecosensitive design (including Peter's Potty, an off-the-grid bathroom facility using compostable toilets that recycle fertilizer into gray water for the gardens); sometimes you'll get a peek at the upstairs functional wet labs and dormitories. To make it layperson-friendlier, scientists occasionally give talks and presentations. The Dive with a Researcher program (where you actually help survey and assess environmental impact and eco-system health, depending on that week's focus) is hugely popular. ⊠ *North Side* ☎ *345/948–1094* ⊕ *www.reefresearch.org.*

Beaches

The southwest part of the island seems like one giant beach; this is where virtually all the resorts sit, serenely facing Preston Bay and South Hole Sound. But there are several other unspoiled, usually deserted strands that beckon beachcombers, all the sand having the same delicate hue of Cristal Champagne and just as apt to make you feel giddy.

Blossom Village Park

BEACH—SIGHT | Developed by the local chapter of the National Trust, the site of the first, albeit temporary, Cayman Islands settlement, in the 1660s, is lined with traditional cottages. Bricks are dedicated to old-time residents and longtime repeat guests. There are picnic tables, a playground, and a dock. The beach is small but has plenty of shade trees, good snorkeling, and calm water. **Amenities:** none. **Best for:** snorkeling; swimming.

★ Owen Island

BEACH—SIGHT | This private, forested island can be reached by row-boat, kayak, or an ambitious 200-yard swim. Anyone is welcome to come across and enjoy the deserted beaches and excellent snorkeling as well as fly-fishing. Nudity is forbidden as "idle and disorderly" in the Cayman Islands, though that doesn't always stop skinny-dippers (who may not realize they can be seen quite easily from shore). **Amenities:** none. **Best for:** fishing; snorkeling; solitude; swimming.

★ Point of Sand

BEACH—SIGHT | Stretching over a mile on the island's easternmost point, this secluded beach is great for wading, shell collecting, and snorkeling. On a clear day you can see 7 miles (11 km) to Cayman Brac. The beach serves as a green- and loggerhead turtle nesting site in spring, and a mosaic of coral gardens blooms just offshore. It's magical, especially at moonrise, when it earns its nickname, Lovers' Beach. There's a palapa for shade but no

facilities. The current can be strong, so watch the kids carefully.
Amenities: none. **Best for:** snorkeling; solitude; sunset; walking.

Restaurants

In addition to the well-regarded restaurant at Pirates Point, Little
Cayman Beach Resort and Southern Cross Club both have restaurants (and accept nonguests pending availability).

Hungry Iguana

$$$ | **ECLECTIC** | The closest thing to a genuine sports bar and night-
club on Little Cayman, the Iggy caters to the aquatically minded
set with a marine mural, wood-plank floors, mounted trophy sail-
fish, lots of fishing caps, and yummy fresh seafood. Conch fritters
are near definitive, while lionfish fingers—when available—with
jerk mayo are mouth- and eye-watering. **Known for:** boisterous
atmosphere by Little Cayman standards; fun, (reasonably) cheap
theme nights; surprisingly decent Indian dishes. ⑤ *Average main:*
$26 ⊠ *Paradise Villas, Guy Banks Rd., Blossom Village* ☎ *345/948–*
0007 ⊕ *www.paradisevillas.com* ◎ *No dinner Sun.*

★ Pirates Point Restaurant

$$$$ | **ECLECTIC** | Susan Howard continues the tradition of her
mother (the beloved late, irrepressible Gladys Howard), offering
Texas-style and Texas-size hospitality at her ravishing little resort.
Guests have first privilege, but the kitchen can usually accommodate an extra couple or two; advance reservations are both a must
and a courtesy on this island, where nearly everything is imported
at great cost and effort. **Known for:** jovial atmosphere; fine dining;
popular sushi nights with ultrafresh fish. ⑤ *Average main: $40*
⊠ *Pirates Point Resort, Preston Bay* ☎ *345/948–1010* ⊕ *www.*
piratespointresort.com ◎ *Closed Sept.–mid-Oct. No lunch.*

Hotels

The Club at Little Cayman

$$ | **RENTAL** | These ultramodern, luxurious, three-bedroom condos
are Little Cayman's nicest units, though only five are usually
included in the rental pool. **Pros:** luxurious digs; lovely beach; hot
tub. **Cons:** housekeeping not included (mandatory fee); rear guest
bedrooms dark and somewhat cramped; handsome but heavy
old-fashioned decor. ⑤ *Rooms from: $311* ⊠ *South Hole Sound*
☎ *345/948–1033, 727/323–8727, 888/756–7400* ⊕ *www.theclubat-*
littlecayman.com ⇨ *8 condos* ◎ *No meals.*

Although it has only 40 rooms, Little Cayman Beach Resort is the island's largest resort.

Conch Club Condos

$$ | RENTAL | FAMILY | The handsome oceanfront development grafts Caribbean-style gingerbread onto New England maritime architecture with gables and dormers. **Pros:** splendid views; gorgeous beach; complimentary airport transfers, bicycles, and kayaks. **Cons:** long walk to nearby restaurants; dated decor; housekeeping surcharge. *⑤ Rooms from: $350 ⊠ Blossom Village ☎ 345/948–1026, 561/283–1715 from U.S. ⊕ conchclubcaymans.com ⟿ 18 2-bedroom condos, 2 3-bedroom condos ❑ No meals.*

Little Cayman Beach Resort

$$$ | RESORT | FAMILY | This two-story hotel, the island's largest, offers modern facilities in a boutique setting. **Pros:** rates include breakfast and dinner; glorious LED-lit pool; great bone- and deep-sea fishing. **Cons:** less intimate than other resorts; tiny patios; bike rental fee. *⑤ Rooms from: $434 ⊠ Blossom Village ☎ 345/948–1033, 855/485–0022 toll-free ⊕ www.littlecayman.com ⟿ 40 rooms ❑ Free Breakfast.*

Paradise Villas

$ | RENTAL | Cozy, sunny, one-bedroom units with beachfront terraces and hammocks are simply but immaculately appointed with rattan furnishings, marine artwork, painted driftwood, and bright abstract fabrics. **Pros:** friendly staff; good value, especially online deals and dive packages; complimentary bike rentals. **Cons:** poky beach; small bike rental fee; off-site dive shop. *⑤ Rooms from: $229 ⊠ South Hole Sound ☎ 345/948–0001, 877/322–9626*

Iggin' Out

An estimated 2,000 prehistoric-looking Little Cayman rock iguanas roam the island, by far the largest population in Cayman. The late Gladys Howard, former chair of the Little Cayman committee of the nonprofit National Trust for the Cayman Islands, took the good fight for the boobies and applied it to the "iggies." Visitors can feed these large (up to 5 feet), fierce-looking but docile vegetarians by hand at the residential Mahogany Bay neighborhood, where the creatures' preferred delicacies—fruit trees and flowers from bananas and papayas to hibiscus—flourish. But Gladys's cohorts hope to purchase more coastal land to serve as a nesting sanctuary. She knew it's a crucial component of ecotourism and, noting how the same species has all but disappeared on the Brac (while the blue iguana still faces extinction on Grand Cayman), said, "We want to avoid that fate. We must preserve them because so few of that species remain on our planet."

⊕ *www.paradisevillas.com* ⊙ *Closed mid-Sept.–late Oct.* ↦ *12 villas* ⦿ *No meals.*

★ Pirates Point Resort

$$$$ | RESORT | Comfortable rooms and fine cuisine make this hideaway nestled between seagrape and casuarina pines on a sweep of sand one of Little Cayman's best properties. **Pros:** fabulous food; fantastic beach; dynamic dive program. **Cons:** tasteful rooms are fairly spare; occasional Internet problems; still some units without a/c. ⑤ *Rooms from: $520* ⊠ *Pirates Point* ☎ *345/948–1010* ⊕ *www.piratespointresort.com* ⊙ *Closed Sept.–mid-Oct.* ↦ *11 rooms* ⦿ *All-inclusive.*

★ Southern Cross Club

$$$$ | RESORT | Little Cayman's first resort was founded in the 1950s as a private fishing club by the CEO of Sears-Roebuck and CFO of General Motors, and its focus is still on fishing and diving in a barefoot luxury environment. **Pros:** free use of kayaks and snorkel gear; splendiferous beach; international staff tells of globe-trotting exploits. **Cons:** not child-friendly (though families can rent a cottage); Wi-Fi not available in some rooms and spotty elsewhere; rooms include all meals but not drinks. ⑤ *Rooms from: $798* ⊠ *South Hole Sound* ☎ *345/948–1099, 800/899–2582* ⊕ *www.southerncrossclub.com* ⊙ *Closed mid-Sept.–mid-Oct.* ↦ *13 units* ⦿ *Free Breakfast.*

⚡ Activities

Little Cayman is a recreational paradise on land and especially underwater, with world-class diving, light-tackle angling, and bird-watching the star attractions. Befitting an ecocentric destination, nature owns the island, and you're strictly cautioned about dos and don'ts. But lectures are given with a smile, and then you're free to explore this zoo without cages, and aquarium without tanks.

BIRD-WATCHING

Little Cayman offers bountiful bird-watching, with more than 200 indigenous and migrant species on vibrant display, including red-footed boobies, frigate birds, and West Indian whistling ducks. Unspoiled wetland blankets more than 40% of the island, and elevated viewing platforms (carefully crafted from local wood to blend harmoniously with the environment) permit undisturbed observation—but then, it's hard to find an area that doesn't host flocks of warblers and waterfowl. Brochures with maps are available at the hotels for self-guided bird-watching tours.

BEST BIRD-WATCHING SITES

Several spots are noteworthy for the variety of bird life. The premier spot is the Booby Pond Nature Reserve. *For more information, see Sights.*

The splendid wetland **Grape Tree Ponds,** on the North Side, is great for observing West Indian whistling ducks and has some lovely shore walks.

Jackson's Pond, off the north coast near Jackson's Point, is a vast mangrove-fringed body of water offering excellent viewing of herons, ducks, rails, stilt, plovers, and sandpipers.

There's more than just fishing at **Tarpon Lake,** off Guy Banks Road. A long deck extends into the writhing tangle of red mangrove roots, where white herons, ospreys, and whistling ducks dive-bomb for fiddler crabs and mosquito fish skittering through the brackish water alongside sun-silvered pirouetting tarpon.

The **West End Lighthouse** at West End Point, off Mahogany Bay, offers magnificent sunset views and serves as arrivals check-in for migratory shorebirds.

The **Westerly Ponds,** shallow wading pools in the ironshore by Preston Bay, are lined by low buttonwood trees and herbaceous vegetation where killdeer, willet, black-necked stilt, and American coot perform an aerial ballet.

Bloody Bay Wall plunges 2,000 meters (over 6,000 feet) to the seafloor.

National Trust

BIRD WATCHING | The National Trust for the Cayman Islands was established in 1987 with the purpose of preserving natural environments and places of historic significance for present and future generations of the Cayman Islands. ⊕ *www.itsyourstoexplore. com, www.nationaltrust.org.ky.*

DIVING AND SNORKELING

A gaudy, voluptuous tumble of marine life—lumbering grouper to fleet guppies, massive manta rays to miniature wrasse, sharks to stingrays, blue chromis to Bermuda chubs, puffers to parrotfish— parades its finery through the pyrotechnic coral reefs like a watery Main Street on Saturday night. Gaping gorges, vaulting pinnacles, plunging walls, chutes, arches, and vertical chimneys create a virtual underwater city, festooned with fiery sponges and sensuously waving gorgonians draped like come-hither courtesans over limestone settees.

Expect to pay around $105–$110 for a two-tank boat dive and $25–$30 for a snorkeling trip. The island is small and susceptible to wind, so itineraries can change like a sudden gust.

DIVE AND SNORKEL SITES

Snorkelers will delight in taking Nancy's Cup of Tea or "scaling" Mike's Mountain, as well as enjoying Eagle Ray Roundup, Three Fathom Wall, and Owen Island. The areas around the East End are difficult to access from shore due to the jagged ironshore (boats are often preferable) but are worthwhile: Mary's Bay, Snipe Point, and Lighthouse Reef (which has stunning Brac vistas).

Two of Little Cayman's dive sites (Bloody Bay Wall and Jackson Wall) are so spectacular that they easily rank among the world's top dives. *For more information see Sights.*

Among the many other superlative dive sites are the Great Wall, the Meadows, the Zoo, Coconut Walk Wall, School Bus Stop, Sarah's Set, Black Hole, Mixing Bowl, Charlie's Chimneys, and Blacktip Boulevard.

RECOMMENDED OPERATORS

Little Cayman Divers
SCUBA DIVING | This is a personable, experienced outfit that often customizes trips on its 42-foot Newton *Sea-esta*. ⊠ *Conch Club, Blossom Village* ☎ *345/928–1624* ⊕ *www.littlecaymandivers.com*.

Pirates Point Dive Resort
SCUBA DIVING | This popular resort has fully outfitted 42-foot Newtons with dive masters who excel at finding odd and rare creatures, and encourage computer diving so you can stay down longer. ⊠ *Pirates Point Resort* ☎ *345/948–1010* ⊕ *www.pirates-pointresort.com*.

Reef Divers
SCUBA DIVING | Little Cayman Beach Resort's outfitter offers valet service and a full complement of courses, with nitrox a specialty. The custom Newton boats include AEDs (defibrillators) and padded camera tables for protection. ⊠ *Little Cayman Beach Resort, Blossom Village* ☎ *345/948–1033* ⊕ *www.littlecayman.com*.

Southern Cross Club
SCUBA DIVING | Each boat (spanking new Newtons added in 2017) has its own dock and takes 12 divers max. The outfit has good specialty courses and mandates computer diving. ⊠ *Southern Cross Club, 73 Guy Banks Rd., South Hole Sound* ☎ *345/948–1099, 800/899–2582* ⊕ *www.southerncrossclub.com*.

FISHING

Bloody Bay is equally celebrated for fishing and diving, and the flats and shallows including South Hole Sound Lagoon across from Owen Island, Tarpon Lake, and the Charles Bight Rosetta Flats offer phenomenal light-tackle and fly-fishing action: surprisingly large tarpon, small bonefish, and permit (a large fish related to pompano) weighing up to 35 pounds. Superior deep-sea fishing is available right offshore for game fish including blue marlin, dolphin, wahoo, tuna, and barracuda.

Art Dive

The bar at Pirates Point typifies the fun, funky sensibility of the dive set, who adorn their favorite resorts with painted stones and driftwood. Here you'll find an idiosyncratic, imaginative gallery of mobiles, painted sandals, coconut fronds, and found art. An old oar fashioned into the likeness of a Caymanian lizard might read "Texas Roadkill Dive Club"; sculpted penguins say "We don't know how we got here but we know we're not leaving." The late founder Gladys Howard created an annual competition for best creation, with prizes including free stays. The staff provides brushes, paints, and a hot-glue gun; guests canvas for raw materials on the shore. One recent winner was a lionfish created from palm fronds and sea sponges.

MAM's Tours

FISHING | This reliable company is run by energetic local Maxine McCoy Moore, who comes from fishing royalty of sorts (she, her mum, dad, and five brothers ran McCoy's Diving and Fishing Resort). Deep-sea fishing costs $125 per hour for up to four people; those angling for tarpon and bonefish pay $50 per hour ($75 per couple). Maxine also runs snorkeling trips to Owen Island and will take you conching in season. She's spending more time on Cayman Brac, so call in advance to ensure she'll be on island. ⊠ 65 Mahogany Bay, Candle Rd., West End ☎ 345/948–0104, 345/917–4582.

★ Southern Cross Club

FISHING | This Caribbean chic resort across from Owen Island offers light-tackle and deep-sea fishing trips with a knowledgeable, enthusiastic staff (book in advance, even as a hotel guest). There's even a skiff with a poling tower to spot the more elusive fish. ⊠ Southern Cross Club, 73 Guy Banks Dr., South Hole Sound ☎ 345/948–1099, 800/899–2582 ⊕ www.southerncrossclub.com.

HIKING

Flat Little Cayman is better suited to biking, but there are a few jaunts, notably the **Salt Rocks Nature Trail,** where you pass ancient mule pens, abandoned phosphate mines, and the rusting tracks of the original narrow-gauge railway now alive with a profusion of flowering cacti and scrub brush.

Index

V

W

Photo Credits

Notes

Notes

Notes

Notes